The Battle for IITs

A Defense of Meritocracy

The Battle for IITs

A Defense of Meritocracy

Rajiv Malhotra and Vijaya Viswanathan

OCCAM | An Imprint of **BluOne Ink**

Published by BluOne Ink LLP
306, Tower-I, Assotech Business Cresterra,
Plot No. 22, Sector 135, Noida, U.P. India
Website: www.bluone.ink
Email: publisher@bluone.ink

Title: *The Battle for IITs: A Defense of Meritocracy*
Authors: Rajiv Malhotra and Vijaya Viswanathan

ISBN: 978-93-92209-31-4

First Impression: 2023

Printed in India

OCCAM | An Imprint of **BluOne Ink**

Contents

Introduction

About this Book

This book is part of a series that started with the flagship *Snakes in the Ganga: Breaking India 2.0* in September 2022. The present volume focuses on the American project led by Harvard University to dismantle the Indian Institutes of Technology (IITs) and other institutions of excellence in India, by claiming that they propagate structural casteism.

While it is beyond the scope of this book to discuss in detail Marxism, Postmodernism and other European intellectual movements of the last 150 years, the fact is that these movements have influenced what has culminated in this current battle against the IITs. Simply put, we will show that:

- The IITs are under attack.
- There are legal implications of this attack. It has severe consequences for the IITs, its students and faculty, India, and engineering education.
- The consequences of this attack will follow the IIT engineer and other tech professionals to their workplace anywhere in the world.
- Harvard's Woke machinery is behind this attack and we need to understand the sophistication that backs it.
- Our evidence-based rebuttal gives IITians and other engineers the toolkit to tackle false accusations of being casteist bigots.

We end with a call to action by IITians and other stakeholders.

Background

The dismantling of Indian educational institutions began over a decade ago with some innocent seeming work on cultural capital done by a French think tank in New Delhi in partnership with the Delhi School of Economics (DSE). Satish Deshpande, professor of sociology at the DSE, wrote a pivotal paper that was published in the *Economic & Political Weekly* in 2013. This provided the meta-narrative that the general category in India's reservation system is a euphemism for upper castes' category, and the need to dismantle the education system. By 2019, Ajantha Subramanian, professor of anthropology and South Asian Studies at Harvard University, became the dismantler-in-chief leading this effort. Subramanian based her research on

- prior efforts by the Delhi School of Economics to establish the upper castes' possession of caste capital and its successful conversion into 'merit';
- research on structural oppression at the IITs backed by research from the French Ministry of External Affairs; and
- Subramanian's own earlier work applying Marxist theories on the IITs to show a grand conspiracy of how the upper castes have structured the IITs to convert caste capital to other forms of fungible assets, thus preserving the upper caste advantage at the cost of the Dalits and the marginalized.

These efforts culminated in her 2019 book published by Harvard University Press titled *The Caste of Merit: Engineering Education in India,* which has had tremendous impact in the US and India. Subramanian's success is no surprise given that she is propped up by Harvard's power structure. She uses Critical Race Theory (CRT) to formulate her far-reaching conclusions with no data to support her wild claims. Her goal is to show that the IITs and other institutions of excellence in India are oppressive structures designed to propagate the subjugation of the Dalits and other marginalized communities by using 'merit' as an inauthentic criterion of success. According to this view, merit is nothing but 'caste capital' that the upper caste has deviously schemed-up to ensure that their power in society remains intact at the cost of the marginalized and the Dalits.

Ajantha Subramanian's thesis has already taken a foothold both in the US and in India, as shown in the following diagram.

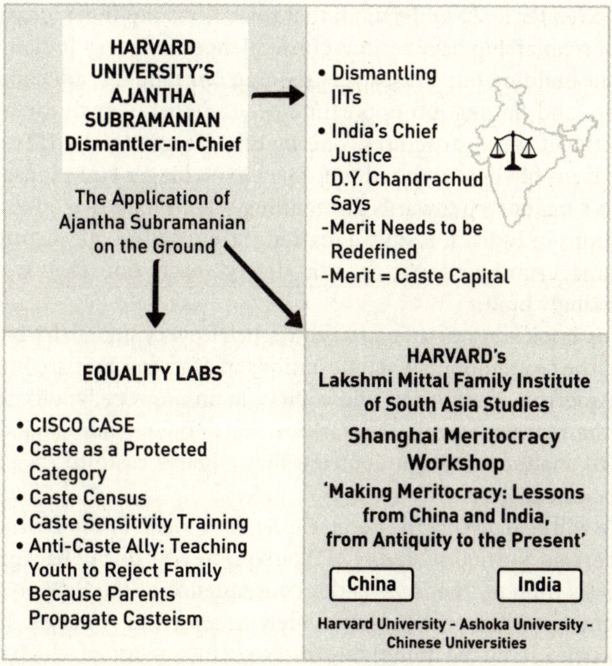

Her vicious attack on the IITs is garnering support from none less than the current chief justice of India, Dhananjaya Y. Chandrachud. In 2022, Chandrachud lamented that he was troubled by unequal outcomes at the IITs, and blamed the traditional forms of meritocracy. Inspired by Subramanian and other Marxist thought, he wants to redefine meritocracy. In 2022, IIT Delhi set up an office of Diversity and Inclusion[1] which also seems to be based on Critical Race Theory/Critical Caste Theory explained in this book.

While the Delhi School of Economics is the epicenter for applying Marxist framework on Indian society in the field of Indian engineering institutions, Ashoka University is the latest entrant that has imported Subramanian's thesis and is finding ways to repackage these ideas and indoctrinate its students. Ashoka is also running workshops and actively participating in conferences organized by Harvard in China to redefine meritocracy in India. In the United States too, Dalit outfits like Equality Labs, run by Thenmozhi Soundararajan, use Subramanian's thesis to prove that Indians in the tech industry routinely discriminate in the workplace based on caste. Hence, they demand that caste must be a protected category under US law.

The reader must understand that toxic Breaking India ideas in the guise of scholarship have serious consequences for every Indian, as we go about building our lives, strengthening our families, educating our children, and finding job opportunities. The goal of such forces is to dismantle all these structures, one by one. Targeting the IITs serves as a high-profile lightning rod to foment even bigger ambitions. It will serve as a major step towards dismantling other functional educational institutions in India. It is only a matter of time before our institutional structures crumble if we do not defend each one that we have painstakingly built.

This book's journey begins with a brief overview of the building blocks, the contemporary manifestations of Marxism that are breaking apart American institutions and society in an unprecedented fashion. Upon the Marxist foundation, Critical Race Theory has expanded its scope by manufacturing a doctrine that equates caste to race in the Indian context.

We will also discuss the book, *Caste: The Origins of Our Discontents*, by American journalist, Isabel Wilkerson, to add to the background. The thesis therein, that race is the consequence of the deeper-rooted phenomenon of caste, has been widely accepted in America. In fact, caste is considered the underlying infrastructure on top of which racism operates. The anti-racism movement, therefore, is being told that it must reinvent itself as the anti-caste movement. In other words, the Afro-Dalit project discussed in *Breaking India: Western Interventions in Dravidian and Dalit Fault Lines* a dozen years ago has now become far more aggressive, because what were previously separate, and independent, movements – Dalits dealing with caste in India, and Blacks dealing with racism in America – have now coalesced into a single global movement.

With this backdrop, we analyze the Marxist thought fueling anti-meritocracy that advocates the dismantling of the IITs.

It is worth noting that the IITs have not bothered to respond to Subramanian's claims. *Snakes in the Ganga* takes direct aim at the anti-IIT forces and gives a systematic explanation and rejoinder to Subramanian's thesis. This book, however, while attempting to do the same, has the narrower focus of discussing the movement to break up the IITs.

We take the discussion further by capturing the lived experiences of stakeholders of the IITs. These authentic voices present a more meaningful response, as they have dedicated their lives to building the IITs, compared to outsiders like Subramanian, that are agenda driven and pontificate from within their ivory towers at powerful institutions. We posed Subramanian's thesis and arguments to seasoned professors at IIT Madras with decades of experience in teaching, research and guiding students at the institute. The response of these IIT professors to Subramanian's claims is discussed in the final chapter.

We hope this book will stimulate further discussion and bring in other stakeholders including successful IIT alumni, researchers, and scholars who have built their careers on IIT's ecosystem, the University Grants Commission, the ministry and administrators responsible for Indian education, and the millions of families working hard to ensure a better future for their children.

It is our sincere desire that the book will appeal to all Indians and non-Indians alike who believe in meritocracy as the foundational principle for building a better world for everyone.

1 | Americanized Marxism and Critical Race Theory

In order to fully appreciate the agenda and methods of American social scientists to dismantle the IITs, one needs to study the evolution of social science theories and political disruptions being imported into India from places like Harvard University. These theories have their foundation in Marxism (mid-nineteenth century) and Postmodernism (twentieth century). The two systems originated separately and mostly in Europe; and then took root in the United States of America where they have morphed into the latest social science movements. Most people who are not experts in this field, however, do not recognize the presence of Marxism and Postmodernism in Critical Race Theory which is the latest popular social movement.

These two prior theoretical movements are complex, and both have undergone multiple transformations over time. This is a vast topic, and we can only do justice to a few areas that bear specific significance to the situation presently at hand. Our account is not intended to be complete, and merely highlights certain developments and qualities in these two systems.

The Fundamentals of Marxism and Postmodernism

While the German philosopher and economist, Karl Marx himself was focused on economic haves and have nots, oppressor and oppressed, the ruling elite and its victims, Marxism was later expanded to apply to broader forms of power that are not *just* economic.

One of the most influential Marxist thinkers that expanded the scope of Marxism in the early twentieth century was Antonio Francesco Gramsci, the founder of the Communist Party of Italy. Gramsci began his analysis by noting that the exploited workers during his time were not revolting and overthrowing the bourgeoisie, i.e., elitists. This troubled him. His reasoning was that, rather than revolting against the dominant group, the workers had *acquiesced and consented* to the beliefs and values of the ruling elites due to the influence of institutions like schools, churches, courts, and the media – thereby expanding upon Marx's renowned statement that religion is the 'opium of the masses'. This led Gramsci to develop the concept of cultural hegemony.[2] Gramsci said that it is culture and the discourse it produces that has kept the proletariat under the control of the elites. That is where the mental/emotional revolution must begin, and not at the physical level of violence. His solution required constructing a counter-hegemony to demolish the old structures of thinking — regarding issues like family, nation-state, capitalism, and religion. Only then could a physical revolution take place.[3]

Later, in Germany another vibrant group known as the Frankfurt School emerged during the Second World War, and its leaders developed what became known as 'Critical Theory'. From the mid-1920s onwards, its prominent leaders — Max Horkheimer, Theodor Adorno, and Herbert Marcuse — were frustrated with classical Marxism. Marxists had earlier celebrated their success in the Russian Revolution in the early twentieth century, in which Lenin led a peasant uprising to overthrow Czar Nicholas II. But in Germany, predictions of a similar revolution did not materialize despite severe economic depression and exploitation by the elites. The German masses did not mobilize against the state as in the case of Russia, and instead joined the Nazi movement. Why was Germany's proletariat behaving different than Russia's, they asked? Gramsci's explanation would be that the counter-hegemonic discourse had not been prepared at the intellectual level.

The Frankfurt School explained that at times, the elites can in fact prevent the communist revolution by using art, popular culture, and myth to defuse the anger of the people. The masses exist in a myth and their anger can be channeled away from their misery. The Nazis channeled this anger against the Jews and Roma people as the scapegoats, thus preventing a revolution similar to the Russian one. In other words, the hegemonic discourse was designed to maintain control.

So, they explored fresh ideas challenging the prevailing social theories and devised the notion of critical theories as a class of theories. Max Horkheimer, director of the Frankfurt School, described any theory as 'critical' if it was seeking 'to liberate human beings from the circumstances that enslave them'.[4] The Frankfurt School criticized traditional Marxism's reliance on economic forces and placed its focus on the role of popular culture in society. They wanted the following sequence of events: Build counter-hegemonic discourse ➔ Change popular culture ➔ Take over social institutions ➔ Start physical revolution.

The other important influence we must understand came from Postmodernism. This was an independent and parallel intellectual movement characterized by its skepticism of any objective reality; the influence of Friedrich Nietzsche, Immanuel Kant, Georg Hegel, and others is evident. It became a popular approach to interpret history, cultural works, and all grand narratives as being relative to the power structures hidden within. The job of the postmodernist scholar is to unearth these hidden structures.

Postmodernism is based on the following principles:

1. General skepticism about the existence of objective knowledge or universal truths.
2. Boundaries between categories are considered inherently blurry and are merely arbitrary human conventions.
3. Power structures and hierarchies exist in all societies, and this is how knowledge gets created.
4. All knowledge is constructed in language games that are inextricably linked with power. Language itself embeds the power of the elites who have developed it. Hence, the use of language is always biased and oppressive.

In other words, all claims to truth are culturally biased and are constructed by the social power of the elites. One consequence of such a theory is that a critic cannot offer counter arguments against any postmodernist statement using scientific evidence and methodology, because the criticism would itself be rejected as a product of elitism.

Postmodernism takes its skepticism very far and believes that all intellectual systems, theories, and meta narratives are mere social constructs. Science too, as a system of rational thought, is such a meta narrative and does not represent any objective reality. We will later see how this idea results in the disregard for rationality found in Critical Race Theory and its Cancel Culture.

The Freudian revolution added another innovation of great value: the idea of an unconscious level of mind that the individual is unaware of, which requires a specialist (psychoanalyst) to tease out. This turned Postmodernism's deconstruction of all human productions and activities into a witch hunt for unconscious and invisible power structures.

To bring Marxism and Postmodernism together, critical theorists developed what is called the second wave of Postmodernism. Unlike the first wave that dismantled every meta narrative, the second wave *dismantled only those identities and narratives that were considered oppressive*. The narratives that are the anti-thesis to elitist narratives are permitted and in fact promoted, because the oppressed must have special rights. This became the new way of championing the downtrodden, and thus Postmodernism got repurposed in the moral vision of the Marxists.

This marriage of Marxism and Postmodernism opened the door to bring Marxism and its social sciences into Postmodernism. It could apply different standards and lenses to the thoughts of the oppressors and the oppressed. In effect, this new form has betrayed the fundamental principles of the founders of Postmodernism.

Critical Theory became concretized when Horkheimer wrote an influential 1937 manifesto titled, *Traditional and Critical Theory*. He claimed that 'man could not be objective and that there are no universal truths'. The implication being that all discourse is fabricated and presented as so-called truth by various social forces. In the absence of a final truth, this reinforces Gramsci's idea that there must be a clash of discourses in order to topple the dominant ideas implanted in the masses.

A century prior to this, Hegel had advanced his famous dialectic theory according to which every thesis must be countered with an anti-thesis and when the two clash and destroy each other, a fresh thesis will emerge, and the process will continue. Critical Theory can be seen as a Hegelian renaissance for modern times. While Marx emphasized class warfare based on economic exploitation, Critical Theory expands its scope to emphasize cultural warfare.

The French Marxist, Pierre Bourdieu, further developed the theory that culture is a form of capital. His contribution to Marxism was to formulate the relationship between culture and power. He stated that people in power use culture as an emotional tool to exploit the public and protect the status quo of their own power. Culture contains deep and invisible safety nets, and emotional shock absorbers. This helps preserve the status quo of a society. People accept their economic miseries without revolting because the cultural structures protect the power structures. In this way, culture has hidden structures that enable the elites to assert power over the masses.

Bourdieu's ideas have recently been applied to the Indian context in order to dismantle the IITs. Through its think tank the Centre De Sciences Humaines (CSH), the French Ministry of External Affairs has sponsored the meticulous mapping of Bourdieu's work in the Indian context since the early 2000s, in partnership with the Delhi School of Economics' social sciences department, the epicenter of this work. As we will show in the next chapter, this systematic attack using Marxist views on culture in society lays the foundation for making a case to dismantle the IITs by the social scientists.

Critical theorists believe that capitalism is subverting the materialistic revolution by diverting the masses away from such a revolution. Capitalists are promoting emotional 'good feelings' among the working class that deflects their attention away from real-world physical experiences. Culture has been co-opted by capitalism, and the advertising industry is one of its devices. Popular culture and advertising serve as a soothing balm that the ruling elites use to brainwash the masses and placate them. The goal is to channel their energies away from any social and political activism. Consumerism, thus, is the enemy of social and political activism.

Critical Race Theory

Critical Race Theory has emerged as the most powerful tool in the guise of a social theory that has pervaded all of society and its institutions in present times. Initially developed as Critical Legal Theory to address systemic racism in the US legal system, it was then generalized to cover racism in all social institutions. Alongside CRT, some of its important theoretical offshoots such as Intersectionality and Queer Theory also need to be understood. These are significant because they have helped CRT's influence to spread rapidly in every domain of American society and are making their way into India as well.

Wokeism is the popularized, mainstream, culture form of Critical Race Theory. Its explicit rejection of rationality and science, and suppression of free speech, makes it a unique challenge to deal with. These influences have entered American institutions like government, private industry, media, and, of course, the academia, where it all began. This chapter thus sets the stage to discuss the impact on India and the dismantling of the IITs.

Critical Race Theory began with good intentions: to fight against the injustices suffered by Black Americans at the hands of White Americans. But in its merger with Marxism and Postmodernism, Critical Race Theory is on a dangerous trajectory towards a similar destructive impact that Communism and other Marxist experiments caused worldwide. It shares many Marxist principles:

- Critical Race Theory adopts the Marxist dialectic that society must be divided into the oppressors and the oppressed.
- Because the entire discourse was created by the bourgeoisie (European ruling elites, now substituted with White Americans), it has been a hegemonic narrative that serves the oppressor. Therefore, a new counter-hegemony must be developed to topple that.
- The prevailing established order (thesis) must be attacked by launching a countermovement (anti-thesis) with such intensity that both get destroyed. Unless and until the old structures are demolished, all social reforms merely perpetuate the old establishment. Only then can a new social order emerge.
- All friendly negotiations and attempts to reform the system are flawed because they end up being within the old hegemonic narrative and its rules of engagement. Therefore, open dialog is a bad idea. In fact, freedom to think and speak must be curtailed to create the counter-hegemony, i.e., a new biased discourse to respond to the old bias. This intolerance is reminiscent of the Soviet dictator, Stalin. It is present in Critical Race Theory in the form of Cancel Culture that has spread far and wide across American campuses and society.
- The destruction of the established order can only be achieved by extreme intolerance, without compromise, and including the use of violence.

There is also an important point of difference between Marxism and CRT: Prominent leaders of Critical Race Theory have rejected rationality, objective evidence, and even science. An example is the rejection of the biological gender binary of male-female in Lesbian, Gay, Bisexual, Transgender, Queer+ (LGBTQ+) discourse. 'Lived-experience' is considered the final verdict and all rational and counter-debate gets shut down. Subjectivity rules while objectivity is considered patriarchal. Cancel Culture is applied when an opponent attempts to counter-argue. Conversely, Marxism prides itself on its focus on rationality and the scientific method. While Marxist revolutionaries on the ground were radicals and intolerant towards opponents, the intellectuals did engage in rational debates.

The theory begins with the premise that there is systemic, unconscious, and pervasive, racism embedded in the core framework of Western society, including institutions (governmental, financial, and corporate), which results in the continued oppression of certain minorities. It draws a distinction between being 'not racist', which is considered insufficient to overthrow and eliminate the systemic racism, and being 'anti-racist', which calls upon people to actively challenge their own biases and mindsets, and to question institutional frameworks and practices, in order to create a more inclusive and just society.

Critical Race Theory gained mainstream visibility in the aftermath of the recent Black Lives Matter (BLM) movement when longstanding police brutality against Blacks came to light in a manner that was no longer ignorable. These events catalyzed CRT into an important discourse in the media, in schools, and at the workplace.

We believe that while these goals are laudable and the problems confronted are real, some of the methods of redress are ultimately problematic and counterproductive.

A major premise of Critical Race Theory is that rights must be fought, not by individuals for individuals, but by groups for their members. This is an important shift from classical Liberalism where rights belong to individual citizens and not to group identities. In CRT, however, the social position of a collective identity determines the privilege or oppression of all its members. This is not about any individual but the way one's collective identity is categorized and operates in society.

Critical Race Theory projects the Black American experience of racial discrimination as the universal lens applicable to racism and other prejudices in cultures worldwide. We strongly disagree. While in the US, the White/Black dichotomy is relevant to represent the oppressor/oppressed, the circumstances in other cultures can be more complex and multipolar.

For instance, how would the Critical Race Theory framework apply to Asian Americans? Are they the oppressor or the oppressed? How would the simplistic binary system of oppressor/oppressed deal with a situation where a community like the Hindus could be seen by some as oppressors (of Dalits), and by others as oppressed (historically by invaders and colonialists who were Muslims and Christians)? This is rendered even more difficult in light of the fact that defending Islam has been subsumed into Critical Race Theory such that Muslims are now perceived as systemic victims, like Blacks.

Cornel West, one of Harvard University's most influential Black scholars, openly supports the CRT argument that Hinduism's structures should be dismantled to protect the oppressed Dalits. But in the context of Hindus being oppressed by Muslims, Christians, and Western hegemony, one could argue it is Hinduism that is protecting Indian minds from further colonization by the global nexuses. We thus have a complicated situation that cannot be reduced to a simplistic oppressor/oppressed situation.

Could one build a case that the *global oppressors* (Abrahamic religions and Western Leftist nexuses) are trying to use the *local oppressed* (Dalits within India) as a weapon to dismantle the structures of Hinduism, so that India becomes vulnerable to yet another take over? This is a common strategy known as 'the enemy of my enemy is my friend', namely, a pragmatic way to use Dalits as a weapon against India's sovereignty. Those familiar with Indian history will easily recognize this as just another divide and rule game at play.

The Indianization of Critical Race Theory

A major development in the US is that caste has been mapped as race, and has become the basis for developing Critical Caste Theory. Harvard University has brought together some leading Blacks and bright young Dalits, and they have adapted Critical Race Theory into Critical *Caste* Theory by mapping 'Caste = Race'. The old Afro-Dalit thesis exposed in the book *Breaking India* claimed that Dalits are the Blacks of India, and Brahmins are the Whites. This hyphenation has catapulted into the latest sociological thesis that takes divisive identity politics to a new level. The door has flung wide open to bring all American race theories, legal frameworks, activist toolkits, and institutional networks into India. So today, American anti-racism movements are the engines driving India's social revolution.

While it is imperative to solve India's social injustices, this wholesale transfer is exploiting victimhood politics in India. One can draw parallels with the British 'civilizing' mission in India, which basically served as a divide and rule policy to control Indians. The implications for India thus, must be understood clearly.

Harvard has become the academic nexus for this project. It is developing atrocity literature to support the use of Critical Caste Theory to dismantle India. Harvard is rapidly exporting this scholarship and activism to India. It has infiltrated Indian industry, government, media, philanthropy, and just about every segment of civil society. Under the umbrella of philanthropy and development, a new generation of elite activists and institutions are being mentored.

Harvard's Dalit poster boy, Suraj Yengde, is the most vocal, and high-profile, Afro-Dalit. He uses the oppressor/oppressed frameworks of Critical Race Theory to interpret Indian society in every institution. Yengde viciously attacks Brahmins, Hinduism, and everything related to Indian civilization. He has mirrored the entire Black movement to form a corresponding Dalit movement. There is Dalit Heritage Month like Black Heritage Month. There is a Dalit Lives Matter movement mirroring the Black Lives Matter movement. Corresponding to the Black Panther Party, there is now the Dalit Panthers organization, and so forth. Yengde is senior fellow at the powerful Kennedy School of Government at Harvard. While race is the primary category of oppression in Critical Race Theory, in its application to India, it is caste.

A large archive filled with sensational and emotional atrocity literature has been systematically built by Yengde and others at Harvard. Just as Black Americans have been officially declared a 'protected class' under American law, so also Dalits are being championed to become a protected class. The effect is that one can neither question nor challenge whatever a Dalit leader says in the US for fear of legal action or public shaming.

According to Critical Race Theory, the lived experiences of oppressed groups override any objective evidence or logic. The stories of this lived experience must become the basis for developing the counter-hegemony to fight the structures of oppression. Our concern is that by insulating this very lived experience from scrutiny, analysis, criticism, or refutation, one creates greater distance between communities. This exacerbates conflicts, rather than help people unite at a higher level of consciousness. Also, this prevents Dalits from excelling because they end up seeing themselves as perpetual victims dependent on reparations. Most dangerous of all, this feeds the egos and arrogance of Dalit leaders by giving them immunity from honest debates.

In the weaponization of Critical Race Theory for India, any group that can be convinced to oppose Indian civilization is a useful ally and is given the status of a victim. Besides the Dalits, the most important among them are the Indian Muslims and the LGBTQ+ communities. Once these victim identities are crystallized, they are weaponized to dismantle the structures, and provoked to attack in all directions.

Critical Race Theory and its offshoot Critical Caste Theory do not want to amicably resolve the issues of race, gender, caste, and sexual orientation, but instead want to hold on to and amplify these identities as devices leading to tensions between group identities. Sometimes these group identities may be synthetic as in the case with a diversity of new gender and sexuality identities that we see every day in the West.

Critical Race Theory in a nutshell is as follows:

- It is activism in the guise of scholarship.
- Not considering progress in race relations in the US since the Civil Rights Movement, Critical Race Theory gives a skewed view of US society by painting a broad brush claiming that

American society is fundamentally racist without recourse, caused solely by white people. This broad-brush claim is then applied to other societies and institutions.

- It assigns blame and victimhood based on group identity. It believes that white people have designed society and its structures in a way that continually helps the Whites keep power, thus making them oppressors of the minorities. Thus, oppression is woven into the very fabric of society to benefit white people at the expense of minorities.
- It believes in a grand plot that the privileged have schemed to keep out the marginalized. This framework has since been mapped from race relations of Whites and Blacks onto other domains, looking for power dynamics in realms of gender, sexuality, and caste. Thus, CRT considers majority groups as oppressors or privileged and assigns complete blame on these groups for all the ills of society.
- Race is equated to caste, and Critical Caste Theory is now applied on Indian society. Thus, just as white people in American society are to be blamed for the ills of America, 'Savarna' or upper-castes are scapegoated in Indian society, men and heterosexuality are considered oppressors in the sex and gender domain, singled-out and blamed for all the problems in society.
- Critical Race Theory claims that the privileged class (be it Brahmins, men, Whites, heterosexuals) have conspired to create structures in society that ensure their success is guaranteed at the expense of the marginalized. Thus, society is institutionally racist, casteist in the case of India, sexist, misogynistic, homophobic, and patriarchal. For example, meritocracy-based institutions are accused of using merit as a plot to deny access to the marginalized. The structure of family is a conspiracy to keep the heterosexuals dominating, while expelling the gender/sexuality non-conforming. Thus, a case is made for all these structures to be dismantled.
- Critical Race Theory rejects equality, since the latter is considered a sham and a way to con the oppressed fooling them into believing they are getting a fair shot, when they are not. Similarly, merit too is considered a sham. Equality and meritocracy are thus considered oppressive ideas woven into institutional structures to keep the marginalized in the fringes. Hence, CRT rejects incremental progress and improvement of the downtrodden within the established structures in

society because the structures themselves are designed to propagate oppression.
- Critical Race Theory vehemently rejects working within existing structures of society and advocates a revolution to dismantle the main institutions of society.

While we see an application of Critical Race Theory in the Indian social context giving rise to Critical Caste Theory, another ploy of Western social scientists to seal this equivalency takes a different approach, which can only be described as a product of a very fertile imagination. This huge leap, which is discussed in the next section, further solidifies what the Left considers the sinister nature of caste, making it worse than race by blaming caste as the mother of all evils, and the root cause of racism in America and the rest of the world.

The mapping of Critical Race Theory onto India's society as Critical Caste Theory superimposes contemporary race problems and proposed solutions of America onto India, while the work of Isabel Wilkerson discussed in the next section claims caste as the source of racism mapping US racism to caste from a historical perspective.

The Americanization of Caste: Caste Considered the Architecture of Global Racism

During the colonial era, which lasted over three centuries, *varna*, a Sanskrit term that is non-translatable into English, was mistranslated as 'caste' by the British, both for ease of administration, and the subjugation of its colony. Worse still, the Indian Constitution later legitimized this new hierarchical framework of caste, which became a foundation of modern vote bank politics and Indian democracy. The long and convoluted history of caste is the subject that most Western scholars choose to cherry-pick in order to fit a certain narrative.

The caste idea has been further misinterpreted, this time with an American meaning in the framework of Black/White racial politics. The recent entrant to the arena of misinterpreters is Isabel Wilkerson, a Pulitzer Prize winning African American journalist and author. Wilkerson uses the term 'caste' to serve the purpose of describing racial tensions between Blacks and Whites in the United States. This newly defined idea that caste equals race has entered the American lexicon in the social justice frontier. Therefore, what we are dealing with is the double distortion that can be represented as follows: Varna ➔ Caste ➔ Race.

Wilkerson's core thesis is that India's social structure is 'the world's original caste system'[5] that lies deep beneath the surface of many societies and causes racism, both in the US and India. She translates caste as 'a graded ranking of human values producing an artificial hierarchy in society';[6] she links it to race, stating that race is the tool used by the underlying infrastructure called caste. In other words, caste is the deep foundation on top of which race serves as a tool. The following figure illustrates the grand sweep of her thesis.

This thesis has gained Wilkerson prominence as a public intellectual in the US and breathed new life into the discourse on American racism. The television personality, Oprah Winfrey boosted the sales of Wilkerson's book *Caste: The Origins of our Discontent* through her book club, while *The New York Times* made it the number one bestseller, calling it 'an instant American classic'.[7] The popularity of her thesis in mainstream media and in American think tanks has given caste a new meaning, making it a household word. However, as we shall elaborate, this is just the beginning of the far-reaching implications for Indians everywhere!

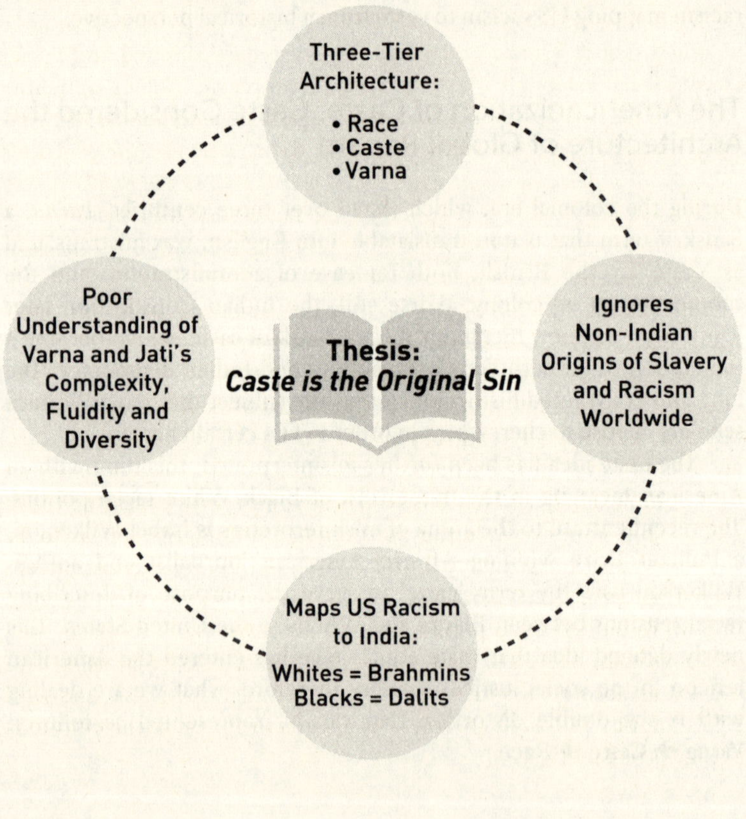

This is not the first instance of caste being equated with race. In 2001, during a United Nations conference on race in Durban, South Africa, the Indian government found itself at odds with a resolution being proposed that caste was a form of racism. Among the arguments used was the standard (but false) rhetoric that '*devdasis* face the threat of everyday rape by the representatives of Hindu gods right in the temple premise'. The government succeeded in getting this clause removed from the final resolution.[8]

But in those previous instances, caste was seen as one form of racism alongside many other forms in different parts of the world. All these forms had a peer relationship with one another; none was primary or the cause of the others. However, there is something fundamentally new and different in this latest claim of caste as racism: In the new theory, caste is the original sin of racism and has been *causing* racism globally. The adoption of the term caste is not merely as a metaphor or analogy, but as a theory of causation according to which caste is responsible for causing racism found everywhere. We will explain Wilkerson's thesis and the new movement being based on it.

Skin color is often regarded as a marker for caste. It is oftentimes assumed that low caste persons in India are dark skinned and upper castes are light skinned. This is used to support caste as being somehow linked to race. Wilkerson also refers to one of her Indian interviewees mentioning the 'Indian fixation on skin-color' and 'hatred of darker Indians'.[9] The fact, however, is that *caste (unlike race) is not determined by physical looks*. This is just one of her many false assumptions she makes to appeal to race-conscious Americans because being Black in America is based on physical appearance.

In fact, most Hindu deities like Krishna, Kali, and Durga are dark-skinned, a fact always glorified in traditional hymns. Wilkerson cannot, on the one hand, accuse Hinduism of being the cause of racism and yet, on the other, fail to recognize that most Hindu deities are dark-skinned, a fact totally contrary to her thesis. Also, the famous rock-cut Ajanta Caves in India depict paintings of individuals of dark and light complexions in which the former are often shown wearing lavish clothes and jewelry while the light-skinned attendants appear to be their servants. These cave paintings are dated before the Islamic era (seventh century) and remained untouched by Islamic rulers because they were hidden from public view for centuries until re-discovered by the British. There are many such examples to prove that using skin color as an absolute marker of caste status is fraught with risk, and such an attempt by Wilkerson betrays her agenda to appeal to the emotions of Blacks in America.

One could easily argue in reverse: that the contemporary preference for light complexion in Indian society was the result of invaders from Arabia, Iran, and Turkey who brought with them the new aesthetics of light skin as a marker of beauty. To the extent Islamic, and then European, colonization shaped Indian aesthetics, and these two forms of colonization together lasted more than one thousand years, one must doubt the theory that it was India's 'original' caste system that downgraded the position of dark-skinned peoples.

Wilkerson gives examples of caste manifestations in America from the Jim Crow era, a horribly racist period in the country's history. Jim Crow was not a person, but an epithet based on a popular nineteenth century minstrel song that stereotyped African Americans. 'Jim Crow' became a popular term to personify the system of racial oppression and segregation officially sanctioned by the US government. 'Jim Crow laws' were in place from 1877 until the Civil Rights Movement in the 1950s and '60s. Wilkerson's claim is false that caste oppression was similar because that implies it was *officially sanctioned by governments.* There is a difference between social practices and government laws, a distinction that Wilkerson misses. Except during the British rule in India, it was not the official state policy to enforce any such caste-based oppression.

Wilkerson correctly states that a problem cannot be fixed unless and until you look beneath the surface of plaster and wallpaper. This requires an x-ray vision into the social problem, and she presents her thesis as an x-ray of the American race issue. Just like old houses have a deep structure hiding the area where the real problem lies, she says, so also American society has the caste system as its invisible skeleton that is central to the operation of racism. Her thesis is that caste is the infrastructure of American society's divisiveness and internal conflicts. Using the analogy of a physical building, Wilkerson calls caste the engineering structure of studs and joists that support a physical building but cannot be seen by ordinary people; only an engineering expert can explain it to us. She is that expert in explaining caste to the American people. She writes:

> Caste is the infrastructure of our divisions. It is the architecture of human hierarchy, the subconscious code of instructions for maintaining, in our case, a 400-year-old social order. Looking at caste is like holding a country's x-ray up to the light. A caste system is an artificial construction, a fixed and embedded ranking of human value that sets the presumed supremacy of one group against the presumed inferiority of other groups on the basis of ancestry and often immutable trades, trades that would be neutral in the

> abstract but ascribe life and death meaning in a hierarchy favoring the dominant caste whose forebears designated it. A caste system uses rigid, often arbitrary boundaries to keep the ranked groupings apart, distinct from one another and in their assigned places.[10]

Another powerful analogy she uses is with the body's DNA: 'Just as DNA is the code of instruction for cell development, caste is the operating system for economic, political and social interactions in the United States from the time of its gestation'.[11]

According to her, the relationship between caste and race is simple and direct: *Caste is the grammar of racism.* She writes:

> Race does the heavy lifting for a caste system that demands a means of human division. If we have been trained to see humans in the language of race, then caste is the underlying grammar that we encode as children, as when learning our mother tongue. Caste, like grammar, becomes an invisible guide not only to how we speak, but to how we process information, the autonomic calculations that figure into a sentence without our having to think about it. What lies beneath each label is centuries of history and assigning of assumptions and values.[12]

Interestingly, she considers race to be flexible and caste to be rigid. Hence, caste is the real problem: 'Caste is the bones, race the skin. Caste is fixed and rigid. Race is fluid and superficial, subject to periodic redefinition to meet the needs of the dominant class in what is now the United States'.[13] Caste, she says, is holding us prisoner for centuries: 'We are all born into a silent war game, centuries old, enlisted in teams not of our own choosing'.[14]

Even when in passing she briefly acknowledges that the Bible has racist ideas, she points out that Biblical racism was based on the pre-existing idea of caste that began before the Bible.

Wilkerson spent time in India with Dalits, followers of Dr B.R. Ambedkar, a pioneering intellectual and politician, who chaired the committee framing the Indian Constitution. That is where she started developing her systematic list of parallels between the hierarchy of caste in India and the hierarchy of race in America. This work led to her recent bestseller.

She regards Ambedkar her hero, referring to him as the Indian equivalent of the American activist and Baptist minister, Rev. Martin Luther King Jr. She cites Ambedkar's interactions with one of the best known African American intellectuals, W.E.B. Du Bois. 'There is so much similarity between the position of the untouchables in India and of the position of the Negros in America', Ambedkar wrote to Du Bois. And Du Bois wrote back to Ambedkar expressing sympathy for the untouchables of India.[15]

All this is true but only part of the story. What is totally ignored in Wilkerson's book is King Jr.'s very explicit expressions of debt to Mohandas Gandhi. King Jr. was in awe of Gandhi, as is the political activist Rev. Jesse Jackson, and many of King Jr.'s predecessors and mentors. If she had mentioned this as part of the history of the African American Civil Rights Movement, it would have compelled her to discuss Gandhi's support for varna, even while he fought modern caste biases. That discussion would require a far more nuanced understanding on her part. Such an analysis would take her down the rabbit hole of caste's complexities, making it problematic for her to pour out sweeping statements that appeal to the uninformed emotions of her readers.

The fact is that King Jr. was inspired by Gandhi to start his Civil Rights Movement in 1954. Additionally, the entire African American struggle of the twentieth century was classified by its early leaders as a Gandhian movement using Gandhi's ideas of satyagraha, or peaceful civil disobedience. Many prominent African Americans traveled to India to study and learn from Gandhi's movement. Wilkerson is selectively attacking Hindu dharma by characterizing caste in a certain manner while blatantly ignoring Hindu dharma's potential as a resource to address modern racism and other systems of bias.

The African American digestion of Indian ideas went through two phases. The first phase was during the twentieth century when Indian culture was seen as a resource to liberate Blacks with Gandhi considered the thought leader. The second phase started towards the end of the twentieth century during which Indian culture was seen as a scourge causing racism due to its caste system.

Wilkerson says that prior to the experience of caste-driven racism in America, there was no such identity as Black people, because their identities comprised their specific tribes in Africa. Similarly, there were no such people as Whites, because they saw themselves as Irish, Italians, Germans, French, and so on, and only became 'White' in America, thanks to the caste system. However, in theorizing the American history of racism, she ignores the role of the fifteenth-sixteenth century explorer Christopher Columbus treating the Native Americans as subhuman people by projecting his Christian prejudices. She writes: 'The American caste system began in the years after the arrival of the first Africans to Virginia Colony in the summer of 1619'.[16] In her analysis, the prior period during which Spanish Conquistadors, with the blessing of the Pope, committed the most unspeakable atrocities on the Native Americans, is not given the prominence it deserves.

She is rightfully concerned about endogamy which means restricting marriage within a birth-based community. She justifiably criticizes many Americans who joined the eugenics movement of the early twentieth century, including the inventor Alexander Graham Bell, industrialist Henry Ford, and the president of Harvard University, Charles William Eliot. But she incorrectly conflates eugenics with caste by quoting the American racist Madison Grant who was known for his eugenics proposals; she uses Grant as one of her subject-matter experts on caste. This makes caste seem like a eugenics project. Wilkerson says that the upper castes in India wanted to 'preserve the purity of their blood, and this persists till this day'.[17] She is unaware that many Indian communities of all strata choose endogamy to preserve their specific identity, customs, and traditions.

Wilkerson seems unaware of the historical fact that the upper castes were also Indians and not foreign conquerors. Indian history has no parallel to Africans being brought from another continent (and hence from a different race) and forced into servitude, except during Muslim rule. Her book is full of anecdotes and quotations from people assumed to be legitimate authorities with no counter voice offered from the Hindu perspective. This is despite the fact that several Hindu intellectuals have extensively refuted the kinds of statements she makes about caste.

Her book applies caste selectively to describe America and show the equivalences with race. She crisscrosses between random anecdotes from India and juxtaposes them with experiences of Blacks in America. For example, she refers to White America's racism using terms like 'dominant caste', 'ruling majority favored caste', or 'upper caste'. Asians and Latinos in the US are labeled 'middle castes', while African Americans are referred to as 'subordinate caste', 'lowest caste', 'bottom caste', and 'disfavored caste'.[18] This is a simplistic way of juxtaposing Indian and American social histories.

Wilkerson says that both America and India were conquered by Aryans, in one case crossing the Atlantic Ocean while in the other, crossing the mountains from the north into India. They are the genesis of the global caste system which they took with them wherever they went. Democracy, she says, has not uprooted the caste system in either country. Despite such fundamental differences in histories and outcomes, both share the caste system as their deep structure. In other words, according to her the Aryan structures of social hierarchy got incorporated into societies everywhere.

She writes:

> Their respective hierarchies are profoundly different. And yet, as if operating from the same instruction manual translated to fit their distinctive cultures, both countries adopted similar methods of maintaining rigid lines of demarcation and protocols. Both countries kept their dominant castes separate, apart and above those deemed lower. Both exile their indigenous people – the Adivasis in India, the Native Americans in the United States – to remote lands and to the unseen margins of society. Both countries enacted a network of laws to chain the lowliest groups – Dalits in India and African Americans in the United States – to the bottom, using terror and force to keep them there.[19]

And elaborates further:

> The United States and India would become, respectively, the oldest and the largest democracies in human history, both built on caste systems undergirded by the reading of the sacred texts of their respective cultures. In both countries, the subordinate castes were consigned to the bottom, seen as deserving of their debasement, owing to the sins of the past.[20]

Nazism, associated with Hitler's Germany, too, gets blamed on the caste system because Wilkerson assumes the Aryan invasion theory to be true. But this theory has been rejected based on evidence from science, linguistics, archaeology, and art history. The following figure shows the premises behind Wilkerson's thesis.

The deep structures of the Church as a cause of racial bias in European cultures are simply ignored by her. In explaining the rise of Nazism, she ignores the role of the Church and pre-Christian European structures that had nothing to do with either India or Vedic thought. She completely ignores how the persecuted Jews found a new home in India; clearly, that would not fit her thesis. Wilkerson diverts attention away from other causes inherent in Western society for its home-grown slavery, genocide, racism, eugenics, etc. In effect, she normalizes Western racism as something foreign and Asian.

Isabel Wilkerson's Globalization of Caste

- **Caste is the Fundamental Cause of all Racism**
- **Caste is Rigid and Different from Class, Which is More Flexible and Associated with Socio-economic Factors**
- **Ambedkar's Interaction with Du Bois Explained. But Gandhi's Influence on Martin Luther King Jr. Ignored**
- **Aryan Invasion Theory Assumed to be True. Nazism Assumed to be Caused by Caste. Influence of Church and European History on Nazism Ignored**

Hindu Dharma Dismissed as a Frozen and Abusive System

What is being omitted in such definitive conclusions is the history of varna's fluidity, not only across time but also in the diversity across communities. Wilkerson makes it appear as though the Hindu social structure is something permanent, like the way Abrahamic religions are frozen in one book. She assumes that social norms have been applied uniformly throughout time and across all Hindu regions. This is simply not the case.

For instance, the history of Indian science and technology reveals that several of India's path-breaking accomplishments in metallurgy, textiles, agriculture, and other fields were pioneered by communities that are presently classified as lower castes. Socio-economic changes caused structural shifts that led to the disempowerment of certain professions. There was fluidity of professions and some that are now considered subordinate and low caste, were once dominant players. The caste dynamic differed in nature during different periods of Indian history.

The pre-colonial, and pre-Islamic, prosperity of Indian masses of all strata is bypassed by Wilkerson. She also does not adequately consider the impact of one thousand years of colonization, resulting in a culture that has still not been fully decolonized. This experience is unique to Hindu civilization as compared to any other major civilization because neither Christian nor Islamic societies were ever colonized so intensely and for such a prolonged period. One must examine the effects of these different kinds of colonization rather than condemn ancient Vedic culture. This kind of nuancing, contextualizing, and historicizing caste dynamics is absent from Wilkerson's book.

Wilkerson fails to acknowledge solutions to social problems that have risen from within India itself. She totally ignores various religious orders that came about as a way of correcting course. She also ignores the fact that some of the greatest sages of India, held at the highest altar of worship even today, like Valmiki to whom the *Ramayana* is attributed, were from the lowest strata.

A more balanced view would acknowledge that economies are never static and there is no fixed economic status of a community. Different professions move up and down in their relative financial standing. Market circumstances, politics and other factors change, and power structures are dynamic.

Different regions of India likewise have had different dynamics of caste. The situation in the north is not the same as the situation in the south. Hindus in the Caribbean do not have the same caste dynamics as in India; Hindus of all castes were brought to the Caribbean and enslaved under the cover of indentured labor. Wilkerson is silent on this. Hindus in the US and Canada have adapted socially to their new lands while remaining Hindu. The Hindu diaspora in countries like Hong Kong is also very different. Hinduism, therefore, is not a uniform, homogenous society.

Another blind spot of Wilkerson is that she seems unaware of the strict varna restrictions on Brahmins and Kshatriyas that do not apply to the lower castes. In matters concerning accumulation of wealth and enjoyment of materialistic pleasures, the lower castes are given greater latitude than Brahmins. In the varna system, there are four separate hierarchies corresponding to the four separate varnas, each having its own hierarchy of responsibilities and rights. For instance,

- **Brahmins** are at the top only as subject-matter experts in formal texts and in the authority to perform rituals. *They are forbidden from holding material wealth*, and most of the material prosperity was earned and enjoyed by the other castes. Thus, they were asked to be poor.
- **Kshatriyas** have political power, serving in military, courts, and as judges and kings. They are not meant to control economic capital.
- **Vaishyas** have the dominant position in business and commerce, the equivalent of modern capitalists. But they are not to enter politics.

- **Shudras** specialized in expertise that is embodied and hands-on. This includes areas like surgery, arts, farming, and so on. They flourished in some past eras and there was even a Shudra dynasty of rulers.

Most Brahmins in the modern workplace are violating their scriptural injunctions that prohibit them from accumulating wealth or holding political power. As per their traditional rules, Brahmins are not supposed to be technology entrepreneurs and wealthy capitalists, nor are they allowed to enter politics. Similarly, industrialists (being Vaishyas) are not meant to enter politics, but many do. Those claiming to be Kshatriyas are not allowed to invest in capital markets. The varna system has fallen apart because the boundaries of each varna's rights and privileges have been violated. These transgressions of traditional safeguards have created some of the problems being addressed.

Clearly, there was no uniform and linear ranking of privileges. The four varnas were parallel and complementary to each other, with separate internal hierarchies. The varnas are better seen as occupational specializations that were initially based on individual qualities and merit. Later, this collapsed into an inherited form of social capital. All these transgressions are fair game for people to criticize, debate, and propose new formulations.

Contrary to the separate prescriptions assigned to each varna, White Americans are not restricted by any such codes. In the United States of America, there are no partitions of the different kinds of social capital into segregated buckets. Whites have enjoyed the top spot in a single homogeneous hierarchy. Therefore, conflating Brahmins with Whites is ridiculous and self-serving, because it seeks to lay all the blame for any social evils within Western society at the door of the foreigner, thereby strengthening Western Universalism as a standard for the world to follow. The schism between American Blacks and Whites is being explained away by blaming Indians.

Wilkerson equates Brahmins and Whites by saying they are considered as the highest standard of normalcy, beauty, and so on. While this could be regarded true of Whites in America because they are projected as possessing the qualities that all non-Whites should aspire to achieve, the same is untrue of Brahmins. She writes:

> A caste system centers the dominant caste as a sun around which all other castes revolve and defines it as the default setting standard of normalcy, of intellect, beauty, against which all others are measured, ranked in descending order by their psychological proximity to the dominant caste.[21]

There is no such thing as Brahmin qualities being the holy grail that all castes must aspire toward. Nor is there any indication in the Indian system of *Natya Shastra*, a treatise by Bharat Muni on the performing arts which also details the concept of beauty, that Brahmins are the most beautiful and Shudras the least.

Wilkerson does not realize that the Indian people, even when poor, take pride in their specific community. It is an identity with cultural significances: festivals, traditions, foods, and specific village deities. This is the richness of Indian diversity. There is a nuanced distinction between the healthy variety of diversity and discriminatory difference; the latter should be fought but not the former. Indian culture is built on contrasts unlike the monoculture of the West. This is not meant to imply that one community is superior and the other inferior but rather the need to recognize, appreciate, and celebrate the differences, despite the discomfort or anxiety this could create on either side.

One can criticize the varna structure as being outmoded because technology today replaces, or at least disrupts, many of the earlier professions, and it is no longer possible to keep them isolated in separate communities. In fact, 'success' is presently considered the accumulation of all forms of capital (social, wealth, and intellectual), requiring multi-varna competence to succeed. For instance, a businessman (Vaishya) who also has scientific competence (Brahmin) is often found at the height of success – as seen in examples like Elon Musk, Bill Gates, Mark Zuckerberg, Larry Page, and so on.

Varna is one of the most complicated and misunderstood concepts once removed from its Sanskrit framework and digested into some other context. As for caste, there is no universally accepted definition, neither uniform actions on the ground, nor a common understanding among those Indians who are ostensibly inflicted by it. It is being incorrectly essentialized as a rigid pyramid of power and oppression, with no variances over time, location, or any other context, and with no flexibility or possibilities for changes from within the tradition.

Ignoring Other Caste Systems

A crucial point that Wilkerson completely misses is that there was no slavery in India before the arrival of the Muslims. (The allegation of slavery in ancient scriptures is based on a mistranslation of the term *dasa* as slave, Shudra as slave, Kshatriya as feudal ruler, and so on.) That slavery was introduced in India during the Muslim rule was evidenced by a major exhibition in 2013 at the New York Public Library organized by African American scholars on how Africans were brought to India as slaves, how several of them later assimilated into Indian society, and how some became local leaders and rulers.[22]

Academic works also describe the widespread slavery of Hindus during Islamic rule.[23] Indians were routinely taken to slave bazaars in Central Asia and sold, the prices depending on the value of labor in the case of males, and age and looks in the case of females. Eventually, after several generations, some of the survivors managed to reach different parts of Europe where they became outcasts known as the Roma people of Europe (pejoratively called gypsies). Their horrifying story continued in Europe over several centuries of persecution. It culminated in the gas chambers of the Nazis – they were among the millions killed although they aren't included as victims of the 'Holocaust'. (The term 'Holocaust' is reserved only for the Jewish victims.) These are the Dalits of Europe, the result of centuries of Christian persecution.

Another inconvenient fact ignored by Wilkerson is that of a Muslim caste system prevalent in South Asia.[24] The Ashraf caste are the highest and claim to be descendants of Prophet Muhammad, or other Arab chiefs, or Turks, or Persians. The Ajlaf are people of Indian origin who got converted by Islamic invasions; the Arzal are the lowest castes among Muslims. The Urdu word, *quam*, refers to caste and is commonly mentioned in matrimonial advertisements in Pakistan. In theory, caste is ostensibly banned in Islam, and so the politically correct interpretation of quam is ethnicity or community with common heritage. There are communities that identify themselves as Dalit Muslims.[25] Ambedkar wrote on the Muslim caste system, and Wilkerson ignores this even though she considers him her icon.

In discussing various systems of bias around the world and linking them to India's caste system, Wilkerson fails to problematize the hierarchical systems within European societies, both pre-Christian, and Christian. European societies were historically stratified according to closed, endogamous social systems with groups such as the nobility, clergy, bourgeoisie, and peasants. A formal discrimination system exists in the British royal family that includes privileges by birth, and a certain kind of guaranteed professional hierarchy; there is also pressure to marry internally with other European royals although this is often transgressed in practice.

An especially dark chapter of history omitted by Wilkerson is the record of the Church in India being established on conquests starting from the arrival of the Portuguese in the late fifteenth, and early sixteenth, centuries. This colonial support for the Church continued during the British era when the East India Company and the British government gave away large grants of prime land to the Church. This is the reason that innumerable graveyards, Young Men's Christian

Associations, churches, and Christian missionary schools occupy the most prestigious locations in cities across India. Even though Christians comprise less than three percent of India's population, the Church and other Christian institutions own real estate of value far greater than the percentage of their people. Besides, they have a disproportionate ownership of educational institutions that bring in huge revenues and facilitate the enjoyment of political and social oppressive power over the Hindu masses.

In an overcrowded country where demand for education vastly exceeds the supply, some Christian educational institutions sell access to vulnerable families in exchange for their conversion to Christianity. The carrot is that by converting, one's education fees get waived, that are otherwise extortionist for the average family. These schools with huge financial, cultural, and political capital were created during the colonial era using native land captured by the British. The main call to action by Critical Race Theory is to dismantle all structures erected by oppressors. The Church would have to be included in any such exercise in India.

There is a parallel argument for Muslim rulers' oppression of Hindus in India. This is about past invaders and has nothing to do with whether today's Indian Muslims are good or bad. Most of them are decent people. The parallel argument would be about the disproportionate amount of land in north India being used up for ostentatious Muslim monuments, massive graveyards, mosques, madrassas, and other developments created during the Islamic era sometimes by breaking down Hindu temples. Muslim rulers also imposed *jizya*, the tax on infidels which forced many Hindus to convert because they could not afford to pay it.

Wilkerson's book has an entire chapter devoted to symbolism in which she justifies the 2017 riots in Charlottesville, Virginia (United States), to bring down the statues of the past White slave masters. She explains that this act was completely justified by Blacks who wanted to rid the symbols of their past oppression. This would have been a good opportunity for her to correlate with India in the way she does on other points throughout her book. She should have stated the fact that in India, Muslim monuments that symbolize past centuries of oppression were built by Muslim rulers to honor themselves. But she is completely silent on this issue.

The reason for her deafening silence is to conceal a double standard. When Hindus demand back their sacred sites and the old Islamic colonial structures to be dismantled, they are accused of committing crimes simply for wanting what is legitimately theirs. When Blacks, on the other hand, take over monuments and dismantle the structures of the Whites that symbolize their oppression, it is not considered a crime, but rather, an appropriate response.

The reason for this asymmetrical approach is that in India, the present-day minorities (Muslims and Christians) have inherited the structural privileges enjoyed by their ancestors who ruled over the Hindu majority. Yet, nobody dare suggest they are privileged.

One should also point out that there is a Harvard University caste system, of which several of Wilkerson's colleagues are privileged members. Indeed, caste-like systems have existed in all cultures worldwide and continues to this day. Much information is available about the Spanish caste system, the varieties of caste systems in African countries, the American caste system, Pakistan's caste system, and even caste systems in China and Japan.[26]

None of this justifies the caste-based biases in India or elsewhere, but the proper diagnosis of a disease is the requisite first step to the development of a viable treatment plan.

Dismantling Hindu Dharma is Considered Necessary

As is often the case with such writings, Wilkerson focuses on the *karma* (work, action, merit) system as the culprit that has perpetuated caste abuses. Karma theory, she states, justifies punishing the low caste people:

> The Indian caste system is said to be stable and unquestioned by those within it, bound as it is by religion and in the Hindu belief in reincarnation, the belief that one lives out in this life the karma of the previous ones, in a past life, and that the more keenly one follows the rules for the caste they were born to, the higher their station will be in the next life. Some observers say that this is what distinguishes the Indian caste system from any other, that people in the lowest caste accept their lot, that it is fixed and unbending, that Dalits live out their karma decreed by the gods, and do their lowly work without complaint, knowing not to dream of anything more. In order to survive, some people in a subordinated caste may learn and believe that resistance is futile.[27]

She feels this is similar to the way the plight of enslaved Africans was rationalized and, in both cases, there is disregard for the fundamental truth that all human beings want to be free. By equating karma theory with the cause of caste abuse, she sets the stage for arguments to dismantle Hinduism.

Wilkerson does allude to some established theories of caste, including those by prominent Western scholars, that caste is a form of *class* which can be remedied for bias without dismantling the entire system.[28] Such a position is open to the possibilities to remedy caste biases by creating better economic and social opportunities for the lower classes. There are several humanitarian projects where people of all castes unite to help the less fortunate, a trend that has accelerated.

But after briefly acknowledging these views, she is firm in claiming that caste is fundamentally different from class:

> It is the fixed nature of caste that distinguishes it from class, a term to which it is often compared. Class is an altogether separate measure of one's standing in a society, marked by level of education, income, and occupation, as well as the attendant characteristics, such as accent, taste, and manners, that flow from socioeconomic status. These can be acquired through hard work and ingenuity or lost through poor decisions or calamity. If you can act your way out of it, then it is class not caste.[29]

What clinches this deal in her mind is her dogmatic belief that caste is permanently fixed and beyond repair by way of any policies or social remedies. The implication of such a conclusion is that *Hindu dharma must be dismantled to rescue the lower castes.*

Wilkerson falls into the trap of reductionism. She wants to portray 'Caste ➔ Racism' as a single, overarching, universal cause of social abuses. A more coherent analysis would consider multiple causes for social biases. For example, could masculinity also be a cause for social bias, in which case it would have nothing to do with India-specific caste issues?

Wilkerson relates an incident where a Hindu man throws away his *janeu* (sacred thread worn mostly by Brahmins) and celebrates this as an anti-caste gesture. She calls this a powerful renunciation of caste. The implication is that just as Critical Race Theory demands all Whites to prove their anti-racist bona fides, Hindus must be pressured to renounce their symbols, traditions, practices, texts, festivals, and rituals in order to be Woke. But she does not ask her Black community to give up the Church and renounce Christianity to demonstrate that they are being anti-racist.

In response to her book, we raise the following ethical questions: Are such critics going too far in blaming the caste system and as a result, making all abuses inseparable from Hinduism, such that Hinduism must be dismantled? Would one take a similar position that because of sexual abuses in the Catholic Church one must dismantle Catholicism? Or that because of abuses in Islam, one must dismantle Islam? Or because of abuses of racism and casteism in Africa among the Africans, one must call for all Black culture to be dismantled?

On the one hand, Wilkerson is very concerned about dehumanizing any group because it is then easy to harm individuals within that group solely because of their membership. But she needs to know that her work plays into the hands of those very forces that are dehumanizing Hindus. This is happening rapidly and turning Hindus into a defenseless people that do not deserve to be treated fairly because of allegations that they are predators and oppressors. She disapproves of people becoming slaves to group think and yet, group thinking against Hinduism is precisely what her work is causing. She is also against the use of oppression to assert control but does not address that the academic harassment of Hindus on campuses is indeed a form of that very oppression.

Finally, the entire movement calling for Hindu dharma to be dismantled ignores the Hindu contributions to raise American consciousness through yoga, meditation, vegetarianism, ecology, and so on. One could argue that only at higher levels of consciousness can we solve these problems and not from the lower levels of consciousness that cause divisiveness and conflict. Problems are best solved by transcending them and looking from a higher viewpoint. The Hindu idea of *tat-tvam-asi*, that everyone is originally divine and there is no eternal sinner, and the idea of *vasudhaiva kutumbakam*, that all living creatures are one family, are examples of built-in resources to help humankind. Wilkerson ignores the fifteenth century Bhakti Movement, a devotional movement that removed caste boundaries across India. This was an internal development that transcended social barriers.

2 Breaking the Indian Institutes of Technology: The Evolution of Scholarship

We will now embark on a brief study of the project to dismantle the IITs. We will show how this has been put together one piece at a time by Western social scientists backed by their powerful institutions.

The French Connection

Our research shows that the French government has invested in a vast infrastructure of research with a goal to dismantle India's engineering education, especially the IITs. We make this bold claim because India's engineering education system has been studied by sociologists with a Marxist lens, through which they view the system from the dynamics of power structures that need dismantling.

The French backed think tank Centre De Sciences Humaines (CSH) in New Delhi is the main conduit for this mission to study the Indian education system with a focus on engineering education by Marxist social scientists. The CSH is backed by the French Ministry of European and Foreign Affairs along with the National Centre for Scientific Research (CNRS) of France. This is a French state research organization and is the largest fundamental science agency in Europe. It is also a partner with the Institut Français de Pondichéry, which too happens to be funded by the French Ministry of External Affairs. The

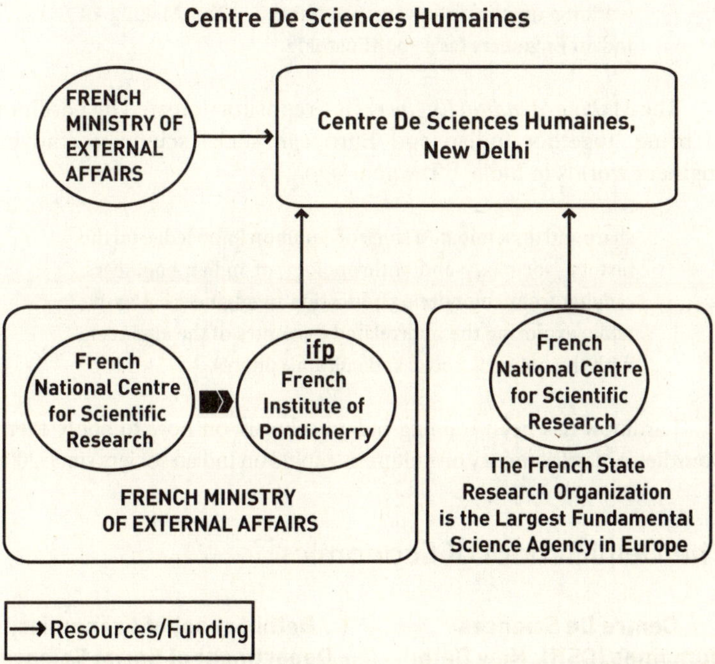

CSH website states that it is 'devoted to the study of contemporary social and economic dynamics in India and South Asia'.[30]

The French government, through the CNRS is vested in breaking the IITs (and the broader Indian engineering education system) with the aid of Western social sciences interventions. We see this initiative gaining momentum from 2008. The French government has been funding the CSH in New Delhi, which houses French social scientists to study India, Indian education, and the IITs. Through the CSH, the French government has made significant inroads into IIT Delhi and is working on a project entitled *The Making of Indian Engineers*. The French scholar Roland Lardinois has been at the CSH in Delhi since 2009. The CSH website states:

> He (Lardinois) is currently working on an Indo-French project, in collaboration with Vigneswara Ilavarasam (IIT-Delhi), which deals with the history and sociology of Indian engineers. ... to study the making of engineers as professional groups since the colonial period until the present time, with a particular emphasis on engineering education, social mobility, gender issues. Currently

> working on the following programs: – The Making of Indian Engineers (as a coordinator)[31]

The *Making of Indian Engineers* is a repository created by Lardinois to bring 'together Indian and European social scientists studying engineer worlds in India'.[32] The goal is to,

> share and disseminate a stock of common knowledge on the history, sociology and anthropology of Indian engineers, ranging from engineering education to engineers at work, while exploring the interrelated dynamics of the engineers with the political, social and cultural spheres.[33]

Lardinois has been training Indian scholars on how to apply Pierre Bourdieu's Marxist theory on culture as capital on Indian society since 2008.

The Delhi School of Economics

Centre De Sciences Humaines (CSH), New Delhi	**Delhi School of Economics, Department of Social Sciences**
• Train Indian Scholars on How to Apply Pierre Bourdieu's Work on Culture as Capital on Indian Society	• Supply Scholars
• The Making of Indian Engineers: A Repository to Bring Indian and European Social Scientists Studying Engineering in India	• Conduct Workshops to Teach Indians How to Apply French Marxists Theories, e.g. 'Reading Pierre Bourdieu in a Dual Context'
• Study Engineering Education, Engineers at Work, Explore the Interrelated Dynamics of the Engineers With the Political, Social and Cultural Spheres	• Produced Many Foundational Papers Culminating in the Agenda to Break the IITs

The department of social sciences at the Delhi School of Economics (DSE) works in close partnership with CSH to study engineering institutions and has laid the foundational work for breaking up the Indian engineering education system. The Delhi School of Economics provides scholars to the CSH that serve as foot soldiers for this attack on Indian engineering institutions by the French government. Spearheaded by Lardinois, and Meenakshi Thapan, a sociologist at the Delhi School of Economics, the department of sociology at DSE organized a workshop titled *Reading Pierre Bourdieu in a Dual Context* to systematically map Bourdieu's work onto Indian society and simultaneously train Indian scholars.

> Reading Pierre Bourdieu in a Dual Context is a collection of nine articles presented by Indian and French scholars. ... Along with a lucid and informative introduction by editors Roland Lardinois and Meenakshi Thapan, these nine articles fill a huge void in the sociology literature in India. Thapan and Lardinois, in their introductory chapter, accomplish a twofold task. Apart from introducing the reader to Bourdieu's work, they bring out the attempts by Indian scholars to apply Bourdieu's concepts, particularly 'intellectual field', 'habitus', 'symbolic cultural capital', 'symbolic violence', and so on. Bourdieu's most striking achievement, according to Thapan and Lardinois, was his 'breaking with institutional divisions' as well as with hierarchies.[34]

The workshop was considered extremely successful, and a paper written on how Bourdieu's approach was mapped to the Indian context. Several Indian scholars were trained on these ideas simultaneously.

> The contributions to the volume are meticulously written, providing a critical view of some important ideas generated by Bourdieu and their application to the study of various contemporary issues. The merit of the work lies in the fact that it not only enhances the understanding of the reader in relation to various concepts introduced by Bourdieu, apart from his methodological contribution, but also brings out the applicability of various concepts evolved by Bourdieu in the Indian context. The editors and the contributors need to be congratulated for the tremendous job so effectively done.[35]

With this foundation in place, Satish Deshpande, another social science academic at DSE wrote a paper in 2013 in which he concludes that the upper castes pose as casteless citizens and thus monopolize the 'general category', having encashed their caste privilege. He says that for others, however, they need to hold onto caste to level the playing field:

> For one section, caste appears to be the only available resource with which to try and improve life-chances in a game where the playing field is far from level. This section, which constitutes the large majority of the population, includes many disparate groups that nevertheless share an interest in caste-based politics. For the other section, which is far less numerous and (relatively speaking) much more homogenous, caste-qua-caste has already yielded all that it can and represents a ladder that can now be safely kicked away. Having encashed its traditional caste-capital and converted it into modern forms of capital like property, higher educational credentials and strongholds in lucrative professions, this section believes itself to be "caste-less" today.[36]
>
> This ... is the central predicament of caste today - its hypervisibility for the so-called lower castes and its invisibility for the so-called upper castes.[37]
>
> One sees the emergence here of a voice and a sensibility that is beginning to believe in its own castelessness. The fact that such claims invariably emanate from the upper castes - indeed from the elite among them - continues to elude proponents. Once they are successfully interpellated by the ideology of castelessness, upper caste subjects see their caste identities as incidental or irrelevant to the claim. They can thus assert with some sincerity that it is mere coincidence that everyone who makes such a claim happens to be from the upper castes. This is the generation that is (generally speaking) distanced from the process of the conversion of traditional caste capital into secular modern caste less capital that previous generations effected. It is objectively true that in the life-experience of such individuals - who, it must not be forgotten, may still constitute a minority within their own caste group - caste-qua-caste plays no direct role, or only a minor one. It is for this group - and this group alone - that family seems to

> have replaced caste as the source of social capital (Beteille 1991). Long accustomed to a comfortably homogeneous environment populated almost entirely by people like themselves, this group is unsettled by the recent arrival of hither to excluded and therefore strange and unknown social groups in their vicinity. It is the double coincidence of the maturation of a sense of castelessness and the arrival of caste-marked strangers in hitherto upper caste social milieux that confirms and amplifies this response.[38]

Satish Deshpande thus makes a claim that caste is a form of capital that can be converted to other forms of advantages suitable for modern life, with the goal of allowing the upper castes to be in positions of privilege. Castelessness, according to him, is the façade that the upper castes use, which leaves the lower castes holding on to their caste affiliations in order to access opportunity through reservation quotas.

He fails to cite any data to support that the upper castes have encashed their traditional caste capital and converted it into modern forms of capital like property, and even acknowledges that he does not know how this is achieved.

> We lack detailed accounts of processes and modalities, the concrete ways in which an upper caste identity secretes and synergises the dispositions and embodied competences that add up to that abstract term: "merit".[39]

He concluded his 2013 paper by saying that future areas of work on this topic need to be done using Critical Race Theory and Feminist theory to deconstruct the universality of the 'general category':

> This is a good time, then, to be working towards a biography of the general category. The problem of false universals is already known to us from feminist theory and from critical race theory. We can use the insights of this literature to understand how the general category has fared as a universal in our context.[40]

Harvard University

Ajantha Subramanian from Harvard picked up the thread from Satish Deshpande's recommendation and used Critical Race Theory to deconstruct the IITs. In 2015, Subramanian published an influential paper entitled *Making Merit: The Indian Institutes of Technology and the Social Life of Caste*.[41] This further developed Deshpande's thesis applying Pierre Bourdieu's work on *The Forms of Capital* to target the IITs:

> Building on Pierre Bourdieu's work on the forms of capital and Satish Deshpande's on the social life of caste, I argue that the IITian's status depends on the transformation of privilege into merit, or to use Deshpande's terms, on the conversion of caste capital into modern capital.[42]

Subramanian claims to show how caste gets converted to a new form of capital that is being called 'merit'. She fills the void that Deshpande left in his 2013 paper:

> The politics of meritocracy at the IITs suggests instead that claims to caste belonging and to merit are eminently commensurable, and become more so when subaltern assertion forces caste privilege into the foreground. Far from the progressive erasure of ascribed identities in favor of putatively universal ones, what we are witnessing today is the re-articulation of caste as an explicit basis for merit. Moreover, this re-articulation is not simply the assertion of an already constituted caste identity. Rather, claims to merit generate newly consolidated forms of upper-casteness. [43]

According to Subramanian, the IITs have been created by upper castes to cash-in on their caste-capital, through the structures established for entrance, in the form of the strict criteria based on entrance examination results. The IITs are thus the machinery that process the inherited caste capital for the upper castes into a modern form of fungible capital that can be taken easily to be transported anywhere globally.

> I argue that the IIT graduate's status depends on the transformation of privilege into merit, or the conversion of caste capital into modern capital.

In the paper's conclusion, Subramanian gives some clues about where she would like to see this discussion proceed. She highlights how equality should actually be seen in two ways, raising a case for reparations for historically accumulated disadvantages:

> The current standoff in India and elsewhere is between two competing visions of democratic equality: the first rests on a formal definition of equality that attributes social hierarchies to the natural aptitudes of individuals and groups; the second presupposes the existence of historically accumulated privileges and disadvantages and the need for compensatory measures to level opportunity.[44]

Subramanian is concerned about substantive equality, which is equality of outcome, versus equality of opportunity. She also makes a case for reparations without citing evidence for how social and cultural capital were accumulated in the first place:

> Meritocracy has been upheld as a republican ideal that is a necessary corrective to older hierarchies of status. However, in bracketing out the social and the historical, it has serviced the reproduction of privilege. Is there a way of recuperating the notion of merit to make it consistent with substantive equality? If the definition of merit could be pluralized enough to accommodate the diversity of historical experiences, it is perhaps redeemable. If, however, it continues to underpin a more standardized measure of value that necessarily favors those with accumulated cultural and social capital, it is difficult to see how meritocracy could be made commensurate with the ideals of republican democracy.[45]

Subramanian is thus setting the stage for bringing in Critical Race Theory to dismantle the IITs, by showing that they are institutions that have oppression woven into their very structure, which reproduce privilege for the upper castes. In 2019, she published her seminal book, *The Caste of Merit*, a culmination of all these ideas making a case to dismantle the IITs in their current form.

Not to have their work hijacked by Harvard's Ajantha Subramanian, the French government-backed CSH scholar Odile Henry, (who also happens to be the director of CSH in New Delhi) has also been studying the IITs. She is researching higher education in India and is particularly interested in analyzing the 'transformation' of Indian educational institutions; 'her future research projects will deepen this investigation on the privatization of Indian higher education'.[46] It begs the question as to why the French government is so interested in transforming Indian educational institutions. Her resume on the CSH website states:

> Affiliated to the ENGIND programme (funded by the French National Research Agency, ANR), she was seconded as a senior researcher to the CSH from 2014 (September) to 2017 (February). As a member of the ENGIND team (Engineers and Society in Colonial and Post Colonial India), which brought together sociologists and historians, Indian and French researchers, she conducted extensive fieldwork at IIT Kanpur (Uttar Pradesh). Her main publications (with Mathieu Ferry) focused on the processes of elimination and differentiation of students according to their caste and gender within the IIT and upon entry into the labour market. Since 2018, she is a member of the ESPI project on the effects, in terms of social inequalities, of the very strong development of private higher education. Funded by the French Development Agency (AFD), this programme focuses on 7 emerging or developing countries. Odile Henry is in charge of the analysis of the transformations of Indian higher education institutions.
>
> Her future research projects will deepen this investigation on the privatization of Indian higher education, based on fieldwork interrupted by the health crisis. In addition, she wishes to set up new surveys on the trajectories of engineers from Indian or French elite universities who have left the world of large private capitalist firms to invent alternative paths most often in connection with environmental issues.[47]

In a 2017 research paper titled *When Cracking the JEE is not Enough, Processes of Elimination and Differentiation*, Henry along with fellow French student Mathieu Ferry wrote a paper in order to challenge the commonly known fact that those students who enter the IITs after clearing an extremely challenging entrance examinations are indeed endowed with superior problem-solving skills in Science, Technology, Engineering and Mathematics (STEM) subjects than the average population. They write:

> As the object of differing evaluations, the meritocratic model embodied by the IITs today should be empirically explored. Are the IITs, and particularly their "undergraduate programs," a vehicle for social mobility based solely on the students' skills, as they claim? This vulgate, spread by the media, which students and their families largely believe, deserves to be questioned.[48]

Odile Henry based her work also on prior work done by Ashwini Deshpande (of Delhi School of Economics, currently at Ashoka University) called 'the grammar of caste',[49] which shows that discrimination in the urban labor market is not restricted to traditional caste-based occupations but also exists in 'modern' occupations. Deshpande in 2010 showed that Scheduled Castes/Scheduled Tribes (SCs/STs) come to colleges with differential endowment (lower skills, and attributes that makes one successful) and claimed that the SCs/STs group had lower returns to education once they graduated, measured in terms of their success in the labor market. Outcomes were stratified by caste, where Dalits tend to occupy the lower end of the modern-day occupational job spectrum while the converse is true for non-Dalits. The blame is always placed at the door of caste discrimination.

Similar claims of discrimination had been made in the West about women's participation in engineering and hi-tech industry jobs. In 2017, a Google engineer was silenced and fired for opening the debate for suggesting other factors that need to be considered for the lack of gender parity in engineering at the company, rather than place the blame squarely on gender discrimination and sexism. James Damore, the Google employee in question, cited many studies to the contrary in his memo. It is well known that a large-scale Scandinavian study[50] could not flatten out the gender distribution in occupations between men and women. Research on Scandinavian countries, which are free societies with no restrictions or biases against women in the workplace, found that despite a level playing field, they were larger numbers of men in engineering and a larger number of females in nursing professions, showing that women favor people-related jobs, while men favor jobs related to mechanical objects. Innate biological sex differences may, in part, explain these differences. A paper by American psychologist, Alice Eagly titled *Does Biology Explain Why Men Outnumber Women in Tech?*[51] shows that men are better in spatial reasoning giving them an edge in computer science. Thus, as societies have favorable policies encouraging women to participate in the workforce in the jobs of their calling, the study shows that men and women become more different in the kinds of jobs they choose. Damore suggested other possible variables at play behind the gender gap at Google, which promptly fired him for advancing harmful gender stereotypes. This is Cancel Culture at work.

Similarly, when studies in India show disparate outcome for different groups in the job market, we must not jump to conclusions that it is necessarily caste-based discrimination at work. These are complex phenomena with many variables at play: urban upbringing, working knowledge of English, inherent interest in such jobs, preparedness, and so on.

Odile Henry builds on Ashwini Deshpande's ideas, but instead focuses on the IITs to show that SC/ST graduates of the institution have different outcomes (compared to students in the general category) within the IITs grading system and with respect to the job market; and hence draws the conclusion that 'IITs continually and differentially eliminate students from the dominated groups (in particular those belonging to the SC and ST categories), and contribute to a high differentiation in the return on, hence the social value of, educational titles on the job market'.[52]

> ... institutional work of aggregation and segregation of populations over the course of which these administrative categories are continually updated. ... while they draw attention to the processes of assigning identities, they brush aside the fact that the forms of segregation applied within IITs go hand in hand with *ongoing and often masked forms of exclusion of students belonging to the dominated populations.* ... The SC and ST students' lower level of success is partially the product of academic inequalities at the outset, and the lack of institutional initiatives to correct these inequalities.[53]

The student placement rate for reserved categories is lower and the authors suggest that it could be related to an individual's social qualities, but offers no evidence.

> The general trend seems hence to confirm the meritocratic discourse expressed by the institution, but this is certainly not the only mechanism at work.[54]

In summary, here is Odile Henry's 2017 thesis:

- Caste determines social trajectories at IITs.
- Claims IITs continually and differentially eliminate students who enter through reservation.
- Segregation within IITs: they have a masked form of exclusion of students belonging to the marginalized populations.
- The IITs transform social differences into educational differences by calling gifts acquired in the family milieu as 'natural' gifts.
- Suggests that not just merit but social qualities determine success of general category students in the job market.

In 2019, Harvard anthropologist Ajantha Subramanian, re-emerged as the dismantler-in-chief of this effort, propped up by Harvard's power structure. Subramanian has all the pieces in place to use Critical Race Theory to make her case to dismantle the IITs as they stand today:

- 2008: The work of French researchers at CSH and DSE to apply Pierre Bourdieu's theory on culture as capital in the Indian context
- 2010: Ashwini Deshpande of DSE shows that the education of reserved categories bears a lower return in the job market
- 2013: Satish Deshpande of DSE shows that upper castes have become casteless, converting caste to other forms of capital
- 2015: Ajantha Subramanian of Harvard shows how this caste to merit conversion happens which Satish Deshpande struggles to show. She scapegoats the IITs to show how they are a mechanism that aids the upper caste convert their caste capital into a fungible asset that helps them get ahead in the modern world
- 2017: French researchers Odile Henry and Mathieu Ferry of CSH try to show that the IIT system produces unequal outcomes because it is structurally oppressive.
- 2019: Subramanian uses CRT in her book *The Caste of Merit*, making a case to dismantle the IITs.

Subramanian's goal is to show that the IITs and other institutions of excellence in India are oppressive structures designed to propagate the subjugation of Dalits and other marginalized communities by using 'merit' as a front for casteism. She says that merit is nothing but 'caste capital' which the upper caste has deviously schemed-up to ensure that their power remains intact in the zero sum game of power dynamics.

We therefore see that the Indian Institutes of Technology as model institutions, considered the crown jewels of post-independent India's education system, have been targeted by French and American backed scholars. To dismantle the IITs would be devastating to the technical education systems of India.

We will now discuss Ajantha Subramanian's *The Caste of Merit* and present our rejoinder to its thesis. We will also show how Subramanian's work has real world impact on Indian tech workers and students in the United States. It is only a matter of time before these forms of Hinduphobic assessments of caste privilege enter the Indian corporate sector in the form of Diversity, Equity, Inclusion (DEI) programs.

DISMANTLING THE IITs	THESIS
SATISH DESHPANDE **Delhi School of Economics** **2013**	**Upper Castes Become Casteless; Convert Caste Capital to Merit** Upper castes encashed traditional caste-capital and converted it into modern forms of capital (property, higher educational credentials, lucrative professions).
AJANTHA SUBRAMANIAN **Harvard University** **2015**	**IIT is the Machinery Upper Castes Use to Encash Their Caste Capital** New forms of converted caste capital, now called 'merit' is used by the upper-castes. Example: The IITs have been created by upper castes to cash-in their caste-capital. IITs process the inherited caste capital for the upper-castes into a modern form of fungible capital.
ODILE HENRY, MATHIEU FERRY **French MEA Backed** **2017**	**IITs are Systemically Biased; Designed to Produce Unequal Outcome** • Caste determines social trajectories at IITs. • IITs continually and differentially eliminate students from reservation category. • IITs mask these forms of exclusion of minorities. • IITs transform social differences into educational differences by calling it 'natural' gifts. • Social qualities determine success of general category students in the job market.
AJANTHA SUBRAMANIAN **THE CASTE OF MERIT** **Harvard University** **2019**	**IITs Need to be Dismantled to Liberate Underclasses from Oppression** • Mapping of White American elitism to the upper castes of India. • Use of CRT to show that Brahmins are the cultural capitalists. • Accuses IITians of a conspiracy against the lower castes and taking it overseas/to Silicon Valley. • IIT exam and curriculum is reproducing caste hierarchies in India.

3 Attacking Meritocracy at the Indian Institutes of Technology

Overview

Ajantha Subramanian, professor of anthropology at Harvard, has written a widely publicized book, *The Caste of Merit: Engineering Education in India*, which claims that the Indian Institutes of Technology are factories that reproduce and perpetuate caste privilege. She is influential in academia and plays a prominent role in the Mittal Family Institute of South Asian Studies at Harvard where she chairs seminars such as *Building Nations, Breaking Communities: The Locality of Caste Violence in Colonial North India*.[55] She is also the Mehra Family Professor of South Asian Studies at Harvard.

This chapter delves into the following:

- A foundational idea of her thesis is the mapping of White American elitism to the upper castes of India. She makes this clear at the very outset of her book: 'To understand upper caste consolidation, I have turned to scholarship on the production of whiteness in the United States'.[56]
- Subramanian applies Critical Race Theory to develop her conceptual framework that Brahmins are the cultural capitalists and IITs their mechanism for the production of more upper caste engineers. According to her, this cultural capital is mischaracterized as merit because that appears objective,

autonomous, and a genuine type of competence. She debunks meritocracy as a veneer behind which Brahmin privilege perpetuates its supremacy.

- Her special targets are the IITs and their alumni. She accuses them of a conspiracy against the lower castes including those working in Silicon Valley and elsewhere.
- The key point is that even when an individual IITian is unbiased, she considers him guilty of benefiting from the institutional structure and thereby perpetuating, and reinforcing, its abusiveness. According to her, by their very structure, the IITs enshrine caste privileges even in situations where a Brahmin student is from an economically poor background, or where a low caste student belongs to a financially empowered and well-educated family. We have already explained that Critical Race Theory focuses on a clash between group identities and not on individuals.
- Subramanian applies the renowned Marxist, Pierre Bourdieu who said that prestigious examinations and elite higher education guarantee the reproduction of old social hierarchies. By citing this, she assumes her case is made that the IIT exam and curriculum is reproducing caste hierarchies in India. But she offers no concrete proof of either. All she does is cite numerous personal anecdotes with self-identified 'victims'.
- Subramanian advocates dismantling the IIT institutional structure and thereby liberating the underclasses that are exploited by this oppression. Her broader activism is to bring about social engineering, which feeds into political vote banks and legislation, as well as corporate policies for diversity.
- Her attitude is patronizing toward the lower castes, implying that they lack merit, and that meritocracy of any kind is a conspiracy against them. What she is essentially insinuating is that the lower castes cannot compete on merit even when provided equal opportunities.
- She ignores that the technology-heavy makeup of Indian immigrants in the US is not caused by caste privilege but a result of US immigration policy that prefers those who can contribute to its society.
- To be consistent, Subramanian would also have to target other kinds of elitist hierarchies, such as Indian Muslims' social organizations, the socialist structures of Jawaharlal Nehru (independent India's first prime minister), the alumni networks of Harvard's Business- Medical- and Kennedy School.

- As we will highlight, her views on caste are full of reductionisms, over-simplifications, and selective use of evidence to support her positions.
- Our issue with her work is that it feeds communalism, divisiveness, and anti-nationalism in India. The divide and rule policy enforced by the British is being reinvented in the form of inter-caste identity wars managed by Harvard professors like her.

The Origin of Western Meritocracy

We take exception to Subramanian's idea that modern meritocracy can somehow be blamed on the Indian caste system. The idea of meritocracy in the West can be traced to early Judeo-Christianity, the view that good things happen to the virtuous and bad things happen to bad people. We may think of this theological principle as *Biblical meritocracy*. It was enforced by an all-good, all-powerful God. Every stroke of good fortune is a reward, and every misfortune a punishment.

Centuries later came Protestant Reformation. As argued by the German sociologist and political economist, Max Weber, this resulted in what he called the Protestant work ethic. In his notable book, *The Protestant Ethic and the Spirit of Capitalism*,[57] Weber advanced a sociological and economic theory that the values of the Protestant faith result in diligence, discipline, and frugality, which became the foundations for modern capitalism. This encouraged Protestants (especially the followers of the sixteenth-century theologian, John Calvin) to accumulate wealth, and many of them saw their materialistic success as a sign that they had earned eternal salvation from God.

In the United States, this evolved further into the idea that free, globalized markets reward people commensurate with their talents and initiative. Because such qualities for success were not necessarily moral ones, *technocratic meritocracy* was born.[58]

The secular counterpart was espoused by Adam Smith, the 'father of economics', in his 1776 book, *The Wealth of Nations*. Ever since, economists have promoted the concept that everyone pursuing their self-interest would produce the best outcomes for society. This ideology pushed free market competition as the most efficient way to allocate scarce resources. Everyone competes for limited goods and limited number of jobs, and these are allocated based on the ability (or merit) of the consumers and the workers.

This historical origin and development of meritocracy in the West may be shown as the following chronology: Biblical Meritocracy ➔ Protestant Ethic ➔ Modern Capitalism ➔ Technocratic Meritocracy ➔ Adam Smith.

Lately, there has been criticism that the US places excess emphasis on meritocracy. For example, Michael J. Sandel, professor of political philosophy at Harvard writes in his recent book, *The Tyranny of Merit: What's Become of the Common Good?*[59] that his own students are convinced that their success is entirely due to merit, even though two-thirds of them are from the top strata of income.[60]

Numerous authors have likewise highlighted problems with meritocracy and cited various reasons. But none before Ajantha Subramanian have singled out Hindu caste as the main culprit. The history of Western meritocracy summarized above shows the logical absurdity of Subramanian's attack on Hindus for 'merit' when the true target of her attack is the Western system itself.

A History of Separating Artisans and Engineers in India

We will summarize Subramanian's thesis that she formulates using her historical analysis of technical training in India.

It is widely accepted that traditionally, technical knowledge in India was the purview of artisans who tended to be from lower castes. This is documented in many works such as those of Dharampal and the fourteen-volume *History of Indian Science and Technology* series published by Infinity Foundation.

The British changed all this because technical education and practice became integral to state power and economic development, and they repositioned it as having upper caste status. Subramanian traces the history of this change that culminated in Brahmins controlling the engineering profession. The rise of engineering was based on colonial practices that distinguished low caste from high caste, manual work from conceptual, and artisanship from professional white collars.

There is little to dispute this part of her thesis. The East India Company Act of 1813 had stated the goal of promoting the knowledge of sciences among the Indians, and the Company's directors decided that the existing institutional structures of education for social elites would remain in place. The turning point came in 1823 when Ram Mohan Roy, the founder of the Brahmo Samaj – a movement that worked on social and religious reforms – wrote a game-changing letter to Lord Amherst, governor-general of Bengal. Roy criticized the proposal by the British to establish a Sanskrit college in Calcutta (now

Kolkata) and urged the government that instead they should 'promote a more liberal and enlightened system of instruction'. By this he meant an English language system to transfer scientific thinking from Britain to India. In doing so, Roy became the originator, in fact the first, to actively promote the anglicizing of the Indian education system.

Initially, the British did not pay heed to Roy and Sanskrit-based education continued. But later, the directors of the East India Company adopted Roy's posture that there was a fundamental error in teaching Hindu knowledge because it was frivolous and not useful. This triggered a debate in the British Parliament between the two camps, those advocating Sanskrit and English education, respectively. In 1835, the debate culminated in the historian, Lord Thomas Macaulay's famous *Minute on Indian Education* that ultimately led to English replacing Sanskrit in India's system of education. Macaulay has been much maligned for creating this tectonic shift, but what is often forgotten is Ram Mohan Roy's role to instigate the process a decade before Macaulay adopted this idea.

The traditional education system of learning was thus replaced by British training in law, medicine, and civil engineering. The College of Civil Engineering in Roorkee was founded in 1847 as the first engineering college in modern India. *The British continued their typical divisiveness by projecting that engineering is inherently hands-on, and therefore the upper castes were not meant for such work.*

They split the discipline to create a two-tier system in their vision of a hierarchical society. For the top tier, they created professional engineering programs theoretical in nature that promised social status and well-paying careers. This was sold as a prestigious white-collar profession and a pathway for Brahmins to enter elite society. It led to a cadre of Indian college-educated engineers, primarily comprising upper caste Brahmins. The second tier was created to equip artisans that tended to be from the lower castes, with modern industrial manufacturing practices.

Some British officials resisted this move, while others were in favor. Those who opposed it, such as Lord Curzon, British viceroy of India from 1899-1905, said that modern industry was a mimicry of Western culture, whereas the policies for India had to be loyal to the traditional customs. Many British officials wanted to champion artisans from lower castes as makers of industrial goods. The debate was resolved in favor of the two-tier approach as a way to consolidate divisiveness along caste lines. By the early twentieth century, engineering had transformed into a gentleman's affair, conducted between British White people and elite Brahmins, with the lower castes performing hands-on work.

This is how artisanship and engineering became poles apart with engineering coveted as high-class and suited to the upper caste. Engineering became disassociated from manual work which was relegated to the lower castes.

Subramanian elaborates:

> The career of technical knowledge from the mid-19th to the mid-20th century is one of shifts from guild to state, shop floor to classroom, and lower to upper caste. These shifts were conditioned by processes at an imperial scale: the transfer of power from the East India Company to the British Crown in 1857, Inter-Imperial industrial competition over the latter half of the 19th century, efforts to minimize the cost of colonial rule, and nationalist critiques of under-development.[61]

> The shift ... also clinched the identity of the British-Indian engineer as a member of a colonial elite who was to embody the hierarchies of the colony. Initially, this meant racial exclusivity. But dual pressures – from England to do colonialism 'on the cheap' and from nationalists charging Britain with under-development – led to a lifting of racial glass ceiling, an entry of upper castes into the engineering service[62]

> The development of technical education along two tracks was informed by and, in turn, reinforced caste differences. By the advent of independence, the status of technical knowledge have (sic) transformed; while engineering was now an upper-caste intellectual aspiration, intimately tied to nation-building, artisanship had been demoted to a form of unskilled labor seen as far less instrumental to economic development.[63]

The account that follows is a summary of Subramanian's explanation of the history of how the IITs evolved. According to her, the two tracks of industrial-schooling and college-engineering diverged and went their separate ways. Lower castes, that had the history of technical skill and knowledge, were displaced and put below the glass ceiling of upper caste engineering. Engineering thus evolved as a discipline of conceptual knowledge in which the lower castes were left behind.

Brahmin intermediaries played a role in creating the notion that Brahmins were innately more knowledgeable and destined to lead. Most engineers in colonial India were from upper class backgrounds. A large number abhorred manual labor, and yet embraced engineering because it was seen as a white-collar profession of conceptual knowledge with proximity to the East India Company. It offered a fast track to the colonial Civil Services and other privileges.

There was a brief struggle to topple the two-tier system in the IITs when Germany offered help in establishing IIT Madras. The Germans pointed out that at least half of their technicians were drawn from small-scale industries and handicrafts and not from large-scale projects.[64] Hence, IIT Madras emphasized practical training in manual skills. But, according to Subramanian, the Germans found the Indians' attitude frustrating because they were dismissive towards craftwork. This was because during the colonial period, the Madras Presidency, an administrative unit at the time, had introduced technical education in a way that reinforced social hierarchies. Subramanian says that by 1921, Brahmins comprised approximately seventy-four percent of engineering college students in Madras even though only three percent of the area's population were Brahmins.

She says that by the 1970s the German model of hands-on education that had been installed at IIT Madras started to decline, partly because of large-scale migration of IITians to the US where engineering theory was in greater demand. Over time, this led to IITians shifting away from core engineering jobs toward academia, management, and the private sector.

The stratification into caste hierarchies was further reinforced when the IITs decided to distinguish themselves in theoretical areas such as computer science.

We agree with much of the historical account given by Subramanian as summarized above. We now turn to her logic claiming that the upper castes cunningly camouflage their caste privileges behind the veneer of merit.

Merit Considered a Form of Cultural Capital

To make her case, she imports the ideas of cultural capital propounded by the French Marxist and sociologist, Pierre Bourdieu, and applies them in the context of Indian STEM education. Bourdieu became well-known for enhancing Marxism with his theory of different forms of cultural capital. Besides Marxism's notion of economic capital, there is also cultural capital which Bourdieu defines as 'familiarity with the legitimate culture within a society'. This capital is about accumulating what is considered the 'high culture' and includes the skills, education, norms, and behaviors acquired by members of a social group that give them advantages over others. Being considered cultured, according to the norms of the ruling elite, becomes a form of capital one can use.

Bourdieu identifies three types of cultural capital:

A. **Embodied** capital: Special talents embedded physically in a person's body, such as singing, having a certain accent, knowing math, or playing a sport.
B. **Objectified** capital: Physically separate from the individual, such as Intellectual Property created by the person but with its own separate existence that can be bought and sold.
C. **Institutionalized** capital: The means of producing and reproducing cultural capital, such as prestigious universities, Hollywood, Research & Development (R&D) labs.

The value of cultural capital is society specific. What may be of high value in one society may be of little, or no, value elsewhere. Accumulating cultural capital can be a route to upward mobility. One can accumulate cultural assets like credentials, prestige, relationships, and networking connections. An individual's family history and social class are also an integral part of cultural capital.

While type 'A' cultural capital is not transferrable to another person, type 'B' is, just like other forms of property. This is an important way power can be held and transferred and social hierarchies maintained. Type 'C' is far more prone to monopolization because its owner can produce and control the distribution of accumulated cultural capital.

Of special interest to our present discussion is that academic qualifications bestowed by recognized institutions are a form of cultural capital. Subramanian's key point is her claim that:

1. The academic qualifications at the IITs are a form of cultural capital of which the upper castes are the capitalists; and
2. This form of capital is considered as merit because it *appears* to be objective, autonomous, and a genuine type of competence.

In essence, Subramanian uses the history of engineering education in India to claim that it became a form of cultural capital. And merit serves as the public marker to hide and substitute caste-based privileges. Upper castes across India embrace merit as a *collective caste trait* to distinguish themselves from lower castes. This is how, she insists, merit has become a way to commodify caste identity.

The leveraging of merit, she claims, is an upper caste conspiracy to perpetuate its capitalism. This is the reason IITians stick together and close ranks to prevent the emergence of an egalitarian society, because that would wipe out their cultural capital advantages. She has taken up the responsibility of dismantling this institutional structure and thereby liberating the underclasses that are exploited by this cultural capital.

Subramanian says that the Brahmin tech community likes to characterize its own success as a form of cultural capital based on a genetic predisposition to education and preordained capacity for entrepreneurial action. She points out that unlike the previous kinds of elites whose capital was in the form of land that was physically immovable, the new form of elitism based on meritocracy, caste privilege, and prestigious affiliation is highly mobile and internationally marketable. Merit is therefore the new currency. The IITs are analogous to central banks because they print this money.

Cultural capital too can be contested the same way people war over economic capital. She claims that when the lower castes used vote bank politics to threaten the institutional structures, the upper castes started relying even more on merit to stay ahead:

> Democracy – as ideology and a set of structures for making political claims – does provide leverage for subaltern politics that challenge the status quo. As a result, structures of inequality do not seamlessly reproduce themselves. Rather, upper caste claims to merit are emblematic of an ongoing war of maneuver in reaction against lower caste assertion.[65]

We understand her thesis but wish to raise the following issues. For instance, we make a similar argument, but in the reverse direction. We have previously argued that the construction of 'critical theories', and social sciences theories in general is itself an institutionalized system of privileges with hidden structures. This was argued by Rajiv Malhotra nearly two decades ago during an important public debate – *The Peer-Review Cartel.*[66] We made the case that scholars like Subramanian are cultural capitalists in the liberal arts because their institutional status gives them special privileges they do not deserve. The following excerpt from that debate summarizes this point:

> The nature of the peer-review process is creating a knowledge production cartel that gives the Western academy neocolonialist control over the means of production of knowledge. Any critique from outside the elite cartel is sidelined (especially if it is seen as a serious enough threat) by invoking the 'peer-review' as a silver bullet. One of the most cherished myths of the Western-controlled liberal arts intellectual apparatus is that its peer-review is

> a fair system. The criticisms we make of their scholarship are considered illegitimate because their writings have been peer-reviewed. ... all our rejoinders get classified as 'attacks' on them, and not as fair criticism, because these do not emanate from within the peer-review cabal. ... those who are not licensed by their academic union should not be allowed to argue against their positions, and certainly not as equal partners. This attitude is, ... part of a larger problem in academic discourse, especially in anthropology, sociology and the study of religion, where it is assumed that (i) the non-academician can only be positioned as a native informant, and (ii) the native informant should not talk back. This allows mediocre scholars to close ranks and emphasize the schism between 'we the scholars' and 'you the ignorant consumers'. Clearly, the peer-review process has acquired tremendous symbolic value. This blind spot in the academy prevents it from much-needed self-reflection.[67]

In fact, many academicians have expressed the view that without a well-placed patron in academia, it is difficult to publish and get ahead based purely on merit. The 'academic truth' in the humanities and liberal arts is often a façade of gibberish, false evidence, and politically and emotionally charged rhetoric. From Marxism onwards, Critical Theory has been very closely linked to political ideologies. Higher education teaches picking or mixing from the toolbox of approved theories and constructing a synthetic argument for whatever the agenda might be.

Proponents of liberal arts proudly claim that they no longer study literature, art or culture in and of themselves; rather, these are 'objects' to be processed via suitable 'theories'. This makes the legitimization and promotion of particular 'theories' very serious business because whoever controls the theories controls the discourse. This raises the following questions: Who has the power, and by what authority, to decide which among the theories on the market shall belong to the toolbox approved for scholarly usage? To what extent is popularity (by virtue of trendiness, money, and powerful backing) the dominant criterion? Does this suggest a vicious cycle, whereby usage of a theory by the peer group of intellectuals promotes that theory and helps it gain market share, a process of assigning value not commensurate with merit? The academic cartel, like any trade union, decides which theories are approved.

This highlights that Subramanian's own Harvard University is guilty of the following: By providing certifications and by its mere brand, it endows its students and faculty with one of the world's largest, and most prestigious, kinds of cultural capital. It, too, claims this to be *merit* and nothing more. For example, the coveted Harvard Business School program touts that the networking it provides via its elite alumni is one of the most valuable lifelong assets its graduates acquire. When students enter Harvard, they become part of the global networking club that looks after each other. Membership into the Harvard gentry is elitist, for sure.

One can list several other institutional mechanisms at Harvard as the means of producing cultural capital: the peer-reviewed prestigious journals controlled by the cartel; the use of Harvard University Press to publish books like Subramanian has done to gain an unfair advantage of credibility; and the highly political process of getting tenure. *Snakes in the Ganga* has several chapters devoted to exposing Harvard's numerous institutions as the nexuses of cultural capital development against India.

Subramanian does mention Harvard's emphasis on meritocracy as a form of hidden bias. She suggests that there should be 'proportional representation' of students and that admissions should be a 'mirror of society'. But we feel that these changes would further expand Harvard's capital. It would, in fact, empower the Harvard elites by allowing them to select the marginalized people brought in and then to brainwash them with their pet theories.[68] Should there be a *Critical Harvard Theory* deconstructing all this?

American institutions have a history of attracting the best talent globally. And US immigration laws give highest priority to 'persons of extraordinary ability' in the arts, sciences, education, business, as well as to outstanding professors and researchers holding advanced degrees. Subramanian is eager to bring proportional representation into all these fields. But would she also demand proportional representation in the sports teams at Harvard and all other major league American sports? Would she prosecute all competitive fields like the Olympic Games, Oscars, Nobel Prizes and other awards to force them to replace merit with proportional representation that mirrors society?

Another massive system of cultural capitalism ignored by Subramanian is that Muslims in South Asia climb the social ladder of Islam by accumulating cultural attributes valued in their society. This involves growing a beard, speaking Urdu with the correct intonation, promoting halal practices, adopting hyper-masculinity in one's body language and demeanor, and so forth. These are identifiers of what is called the Ashraf caste of Muslims, their highest caste. Such topics would be too politically incorrect for the otherwise provocative Subramanian. She ought to note Ambedkar's criticism of Muslim elitism as summarized in Chapter 6 of *Snakes in the Ganga*.

Entrance Exams Conceal Caste Privileges

The entrance exam to the IITs is considered one of the most standard, objective, and neutral measures of modern meritocracy by the youth of India. But Subramanian says the in-built social and cultural capital structures have not been adequately dismantled. She feels there are economic, social, and ideological factors that make the exam unfair to the lower castes. Therefore, they cannot succeed in engineering professions.

She fails to provide concrete examples or logic to prove that the exam privileges certain castes over others. All she does is cite numerous interviews with self-identified 'victims' from which she selects random anecdotes to support her theory. She repeatedly claims that she is speaking for the downtrodden, that she is their voice. But this is a common anthropological device and there is nothing scientific about such a methodology.

Subramanian's argument is shallow because she merely cites Bourdieu who said that prestigious examinations and elite higher education guarantee the reproduction of old social hierarchies. She then assumes that looking at India through Bourdieu's lens, she has made the case that the IIT exam and curriculum are reproducing caste hierarchies in India too. Her attitude is patronizing towards the lower castes, implying that they lack merit, and that meritocracy of any kind is a conspiracy against them. What she is essentially insinuating is that the lower castes cannot compete on merit even when provided equal opportunities.

A stronger case would be that the lower castes were not prepared through primary education because during the British era there was no universal education policy for the masses. This continued post-Independence under the leadership of Jawaharlal Nehru and Indira Gandhi (India's longest serving prime minister). Therefore, by the time these youth consider engineering as an option, they are already at a handicap. This is a secular issue caused by colonialism and the subsequent elitism that continued during the Nehruvian era.

Subramanian is also critical of the Union Public Service Commission exam that admits candidates into India's elite government services, alleging it comprises elitist structures. However, the exam also has a heavy dose of social sciences, and the social sciences taught in India are entirely imported from the West. It is she and others like her at institutions like Harvard, themselves products of the Western social sciences, that have created these elite structures in India.

The underlying reason for opposing entrance exams is her adoption of the Critical Race Theory tenet favoring equity over equality. This means advocating equal outcomes and not equal opportunities. Such a view places less emphasis on equipping institutions to better prepare underprivileged students and help them perform on par with the best. The implicit assumption is that the underprivileged are incapable of learning, and hence the outcomes should be institutionalized to mirror the composition of society. An equitable admissions policy, according to her, would focus primarily on each student's history and identity and not consider aptitude for a given field.

Merit as Male Dominated Capitalism

One of Subramanian's major allegations is that the majority of IITians are male. She further asserts that male bonding on campuses was preconfigured by male relationships within the Hindu family. In other words, the Hindu male hierarchy in families brings about the masculine quality into the engineering profession. However, the fact to note is that in the US too, STEM education is male dominated and hence it is not something unique to Hindu societies.[69] Our position is that STEM should be encouraged for all genders and identities. The solution to a lack of performance by certain groups should not be based on the flawed diagnosis of blaming a convenient scapegoat. Subramanian also ignores the fact that India produces the world's highest number of females in STEM education.[70]

Institutional Kinship Among IITians and Brand Development Considered Casteist

Subramanian finds it unusual that IITians stand up for each other and is troubled by their brand becoming a form of cultural capital:

> The institutional kinship within the overwhelmingly upper-caste IIT diaspora has become an even more potent form of capital. Diasporic IITians have been at the forefronts of efforts to sustain and consolidate their effective ties and to make the IIT pedigree into a globally recognized brand. Much of this work of branding has been driven by IITians in Silicon Valley, for whom entrepreneurial success has further reinforced their sense of being self-made individuals.[71]

However, fostering cooperation among its members is the nature of every university's alumni association. She is unhappy about the success of the IITs in this regard:

> The IITians of Silicon Valley have been at the forefront of professional networking and image making to ensure that the Indian technical professional is immediately recognizable as a global commodity. Their networks of affiliation and accumulation work to reinforce the upper caste under pilings of Indian technical merit even while caste disappears from view.[72]

It is unclear what caste has to do with the fact that IITians like all other alumni, promote themselves, build their image, and help each other on a global level just like any other institution. Networking is a key benefit and aspiration for any student body, an intangible benefit. It is an inherent feature of any modern educational system, and any criticism of this kind needs to lay at the feet of the Western education system itself and not selectively scapegoated upon Indians or Hindus.

Subramanian also takes a pot-shot at TIE, i.e., The Indus Entrepreneurs, a group created in 1992 mainly by IITians in Silicon Valley.[73] The Indus Entrepreneurs has spread worldwide with chapters in several countries. It is a non-profit organization for networking among tech entrepreneurs, venture capitalists, employees, and employers. Such organizations exist in business, medicine, the hospitality industry, the legal profession, and even in anthropology, which is her field. There is nothing amiss if Indians have taken the lead to create the world's premier professional association for technologists.

Subramanian is also troubled that many Indians own Silicon Valley companies and are angel investors favoring those with similar backgrounds. But this is a common trend across all professions: people giving preference to those from the same university, village or other affiliation based on one type of identity or another. In fact, proponents of diversity strongly encourage minority communities to organize such formal and informal networks to break the monopoly of White elite strangleholds over access and traditional networks. Belonging to associations like TIE and encouraging lower castes to build similar networks are not mutually exclusive.

What upsets her further is that Silicon Valley IITians have created the Pan-IIT Alumni Association which too has spread around the world. She acknowledges that this is like the Harvard Business School network but does not go to the same lengths criticizing either that or the Harvard Medical School network or the Harvard Kennedy School of Government network. Attacking them would be risky for her Ivy League career.

Among the targets she names are a wide range of individuals that have championed the IIT brand. These include Vinod Khosla, renowned venture capitalist and co-founder of Sun Microsystems, N.R. Narayana Murthy, founder of Infosys, and various others. She mentions that former and current US presidents, Bill Clinton and Joe Biden also praised the IITians, as did Bill Gates (of Microsoft), Jeff Bezos (of Amazon) and Nobel Prize winner, Prof. Amartya Sen. She is upset about the success of the IITs: 'Lost in this rhetorical echo chamber are the forms of inherited caste capital and state patronage that have gone into the making of the IITs'.[74]

The US-based Patel community is known to help each other get into the hotel business. Sikhs in New Jersey own most of the gas stations; they train, mentor, and finance each other get into the business. Similarly, Koreans own most of the laundromats. This is a fact of American society: When people migrate from a certain country, they stick together, and become professionally specialized in some area. Similarly, there is nothing unusual about IIT graduates standing up for each other, even if, for reasons beyond their control, they happen to be Tamil Brahmins of proven merit. Subramanian calls it 'institutional kinship' and considers it a Brahmin conspiracy to create a brand that makes IIT more attractive among employers the world over. The fact is that India's outsourcing industry wants to market its people, and it is a good business strategy to project a positive brand to its clients.

Subramanian mentions that IITians are treated very differently than students from India's Regional Engineering Colleges that cater to the lower strata of society. And it is an issue for her that the IITs are considered the benchmark of meritocracy. She mentions that many followers of Gandhi's ideology initially found the IITs to be elitist, but later maintained that even the ancient Buddhist university of Nalanda became renowned the world over because it was elitist and picked the highest caliber of talent regardless of social status.

Another point of concern for her is the success of the diaspora entrepreneurs because this has become a pride of Indians. She says that IITians in Silicon Valley have become 'self-styled neo-liberal capitalists'. But this is the very nature of the global capitalist society we live in; it is the nature and structure of free enterprise and has nothing to do with being Brahmins or IITians, or caste in the least.

She is disdainful of IITians criticizing the underdevelopment of the Indian public sector and the underachievement of engineers based in India. But why should she have the sole prerogative to develop a critique of Indian engineers; why can't others develop their own thesis on the problem? In fact, IITians are better qualified than an anthropologist to recommend policies on engineering education in India.

We, too, have criticized India's policies for failing to use its engineers but in a different way: Our criticism is that India is basically selling its engineers as raw labor and making a few billionaires even richer, while the technology produced belongs to a foreign client who then licenses it back to India.

Throughout her work, her contempt for the accomplishments of Indian American technocrats is clear.

Attack on Silicon Valley

Subramanian's goal is to cause fissures in the sensitive US landscape of race tensions by wanting to pit one minority group against the other. She writes:

> ... people in the United States who are really committed to elevating the IIT brand and creating this myth of the technological Indian are also involved in politics in India. [They] push certain forms of entrepreneurialism in India, sometimes through the IITs, but often in other ways ... Some of them are consultants ... And they're really invested in certain forms of economic and legal transformation that allow for more unfettered foreign investment and more deregulation of public sector industries. It's both a project with a U.S. specific focus, but it also has a transnational dimension. What does it mean to be a model minority? It means that you are exceptional and ... can be held up as a model for other less successful minorities. ... your success is pitted against those other minorities in a way that completely obscures the forms of caste and class capital that most of Asian Americans enjoy.[75]

She is a staunch supporter of Equality Labs, run by Thenmozhi Soundararajan that helped build the recent case against Cisco alleging caste discrimination. She writes 'caste is a travelling category' and that caste privilege in the form of social and cultural capital is a 'transferable form of capital' that Indians have brought to the US.[76]

She freely opines about caste being alive in American corporates, and echoes Critical Race Theory to say that the policy of neutrality towards all castes protects caste privilege:

> It's not an accident that the vast majority of South Asian-Americans are from privileged caste backgrounds. ... if one doesn't subscribe to a caste identity, one is still a beneficiary of caste privilege. So caste is here, it has been here, and it

> will stay here. So one has to actually contend with it and not pretend that it doesn't exist.[77]

Ironically, many people of upper caste backgrounds have immigrated to the West in response to reservations policies in India that make it much more difficult for them to gain access to educational institutions, relative to other castes and backgrounds. She says the upper caste Indian migrants' success is not self-made, but a success resulting from caste as social capital transferred from India. She accuses Indian Americans of preserving this upper caste capital but fails to acknowledge that most Indian Americans do not identify themselves with any particular caste and often marry out of caste. If a typical Indian American is asked their caste, in many cases they will not have an answer.

Rather than be proud that IIT Madras has an entrepreneurship cell, she criticizes this group for taking credit for forming 130 start-ups and creating 250 internships. She is concerned that these collaborations between the diaspora and the homeland is evidence of IITians and other Indians having subscribed to the Silicon Valley model of meritocracy. Every sign and instance of Indians' success is seen by her as a conspiracy against the lower castes. Even India's former prime minister, Dr Manmohan Singh, and Raghuram Rajan (former chief economist of the IMF and former governor of the Reserve Bank of India) are quoted among those that praise the IITs, and hence they too, are part of this caste conspiracy.

Subramanian positions her following statement in the context of criticizing the IITs, when in fact, most IITians would regard it as a matter of pride:

> IITians were able to bring the spirit of entrepreneurship to India and cultivated a new generation of capitalists who ... removed the nation's shackles of socialism. With ... diasporic entrepreneurship, brand IIT becomes brand India. This diasporic liberal theology raises the nation's deliverance, squarely in the hands of the US based IITians.[78]

She wants anthropologists and social scientists like herself to be the ones delivering fresh ideology to the downtrodden and is resentful that IITians have achieved more success than her own cabal. What is also troubling to her is that IITians have resisted victimhood branding.

> Equating India's development status with brand value, it reduces the social, political, and even ethical complexity of development to market price. ... the capacity to

> attract investment and accumulate wealth becomes the preeminent index of social value and intellectual merit.[79]

It is true that structural socio-economic factors result in disparate levels of access to resources that help make one successful and be meritorious. Those issues absolutely need to be addressed. However, what is insidious about Subramanian's line of argument is that the very concept of 'merit' itself is being delegitimized. Any differentiation in outcomes is blamed on conspiracy and structural elitism. The natural corollary that follows is that there can be no valid system of meritocracy. The target of such an attack is capitalism and free thinking; this is pure totalitarian Marxism sneaking in through the guise of anti-racism and anti-casteism.

Breaking Ranks with Afro-Dalits

While Subramanian is clear about the mapping *upper caste = Whites*, she does not want to equate *lower caste = Blacks* to the same extent as do Isabel Wilkerson and Suraj Yengde (of Harvard Kennedy School).

She disagrees with Wilkerson's use of caste as the fixed, permanent architecture in which racism plays out universally. Her main issue with Wilkerson's thesis is that she regards caste as specific to India's history and not something that could be plucked out surgically and inserted elsewhere out of context. It is a by-product of a unique experience of foreign colonialism and capitalism combined with internal developments.

Another contrast to Wilkerson is that Subramanian does not want to disregard the social struggles of the past two centuries. She argues that both caste in India and race in America have undergone considerable change, and that there is much fluidity and mobility within each system. The social and political life of caste is far more complex, and she opposes simplistic comparisons of caste and race.[80]

But we cannot help speculating that there is a turf battle between them: *Subramanian wants to **own** the discourse on caste in the American academy*. Her criticism of Wilkerson suggests that she is willing to concede the criticism of race to Wilkerson, a Black scholar, in exchange for caste being uniquely Indian becoming *her* exclusive domain. She must make her argument different from the widely popular Wilkerson thesis, so as to carve out a space for herself where she would dominate as the academic expert.

The Politics of Jawaharlal Nehru v/s Narendra Modi

After India gained Independence in 1947, Jawaharlal Nehru dreamt of building a nation based on modern science and technology. Hence, he was very big on the idea of the IITs as well as large-scale steel plants and other infrastructure projects with foreign help. Subramanian takes Nehru to task that these new engineering colleges were kept insulated from caste politics, thereby enabling them to continue reproducing caste hierarchies. Nehru had even characterized science and technology as something Brahminical in the spirit of service. She feels that this further entrenched the idea of the scientist as an elitist, and the material and physical aspects became the domain of the less privileged, the lower castes. As per her, Nehru, in effect, mimicked Europe by making the IITs as part of the two-tier engineering system.

But she neglects the deeper root cause: Nehru and Indira Gandhi neglected mass education at the grassroots level, which has created the present stratification in higher education. Nehru's state socialism as the model for the planned economy was also elitist but has not been adequately examined by Subramanian.

Subramanian's posture on Narendra Modi is far more antagonistic than her calm reflections on Nehru. She outright dismisses all of Modi's accomplishments as authoritarian:

> The rise of Narendra Modi has ordered another shift in IITian projects of self-fashioning. In the United States this has been most clearly seen in the IITians endorsement of the BJP's neo liberal capitalism. ... Modi's style of authoritarian populism has also garnered support in both the United States and India. ... this is evident in an escalation of cultural nationalist politics on IIT campuses. It is to this most recent expression of upper casteness within India, and its implications for the ongoing dialectic of upper caste claims to merit and lower caste claims to rise that we turn to in the conclusion.[81]

She conveniently ignores the fact that Modi's electoral victories (both in 2014 and 2019) were largely due to the massive support he received from the lower castes. It is ironic that even after acknowledging the long history that led to what she considers IIT elitism, she ends up blaming the ruling Bharatiya Janata Party (BJP) as the culprit.

She is troubled that a spokesman for the IITs praises Modi's policies on technocrats and capitalists. She picks on him for saying that the IITs have been a beacon of light in contrast with state socialism in India. His statement that those IITians who migrated to the US did very well as self-made entrepreneurs while those who stayed in India have languished, reflects on the character of the US. Whether it is immigrants from China, Japan, Germany, Russia, Poland, or anywhere else, the US is a land where people compete on grounds of meritocracy and free enterprise. This US ethos has nothing to do with Hinduism or any kind of caste privilege of Indian Brahmins.

Yet, she says that the election of 'Hindu nationalists' in India led to a reinforcement of caste power that is reflected in the diaspora. The reason cited is that Modi is caste-oriented (even though he does not belong to the upper caste community) and is supporting upper caste privileges. She writes:

> As with other majoritarian nationalisms, Hindu nationalism has long had a social base among the upper caste middle class. Most IITians are the perfect combination of both constituencies having emerged out of the upper caste middle class members to become capitalist class, spanning homeland and diaspora.[82]

Subramanian, however, gives no evidence as to which policies of Modi's government are anti-lower caste. On the contrary, a lot of infrastructure, job development, and several social programs have been pro minorities and lower castes. A good scholar ought to have made factual statistical comparisons between the progress of lower castes during various political governments in India. But that seems beyond the scope of Subramanian's work. In fact, in the conclusion to her book, she makes a list of what she considers to be the great achievements of the previous Congress government in helping alleviate poverty and give rights to the downtrodden; but doesn't provide any statistical comparison to back her sweeping generalizations.[83]

She depicts the IITs as institutions preventing the redistribution of wealth from the rich to the poor, and preserving the separation of upper and lower caste work:

> In the successive fault lines between the mental and the manual, the gifted and the coached, the general and the reserved, the diaspora and homeland, and authoritarianism and lower caste rights politics, we see the dynamic and sustained forms of maneuver through which the possessive investment in upper caste-ness is expressed and secured.[84]

Concerns with Ajantha Subramanian's Thesis

The diagram that follows summarizes Subramanian's thesis, the activism resulting from it, and the impact on Breaking India forces.

Subramanian does not want caste to be treated like economic class because that would make caste biases solvable through economic development. Her agenda requires that caste is a permanent long-term structure, and she wants nothing short of dismantling everything built on top of that structure. We find this view short-sighted and dangerous in this age of competitive globalization. She fails to analyze the broader implications of STEM education in nation-building and uplifting of *all* communities.

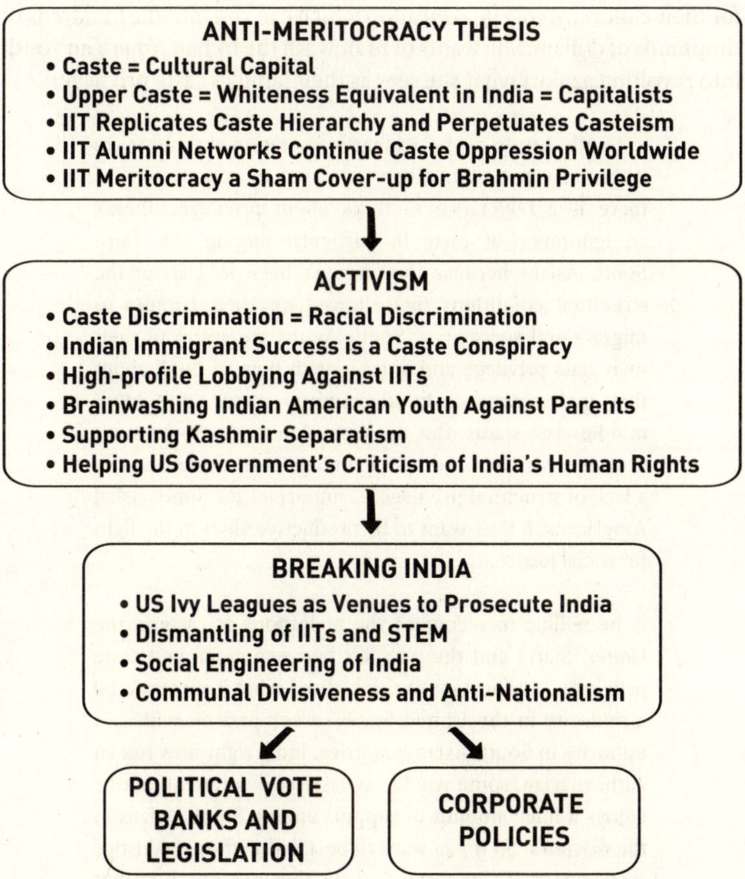

Subramanian totally ignores the hard work required to gain admission into the IITs that leads to the success stories of thousands of students. In fact, *she argues that the very act of defending merit-based outcomes is itself a manifestation of caste privilege.* As we saw earlier, this close-mindedness is directly lifted from Critical Race Theory, shutting the door to any rational argument against her position.

She seems unfazed that US universities are known for Hinduphobic attitudes in South Asian Studies departments, which puts Hindu students at a psychological disadvantage compared to students of other faiths. To make matters worse, some academics like her and Suraj Yengde are busy brainwashing young Indians in universities to look down upon their parents with disdain for 'being casteist'. She ignores the fact that it is common for Indian parents to invest their life savings for their children's college education which can run into the hundreds of thousands of dollars. She wants to brainwash the Indian American youth into revolting against what she sees as their family's caste privilege:

> ... South Asians of the younger generation that do make common cause with other social justice movements. ... there is a reluctance to think about privilege. There's an ignorance of caste in particular among U.S. born South Asians because they haven't been told about the structural conditions that allowed for their families to migrate and succeed. ... South Asians are aware of their own class privilege and grapple with how to think about that intersection of racial minority status and upper middle-class status. But the caste dimension of the story is often invisible. ... (do not) conflate non-whiteness with a lack of structural privilege. ... important for South Asian Americans, if they want to be productive allies in the fight for social justice.
>
> ... be willing to recognize the operations of caste in the United States and the parallels between racial and caste privilege. ... important to think about what it means to be a minority in the United States in comparison with ... a minority in South Asian countries. India right now has an authoritarian, some would say fascist government, and ... enjoys a huge amount of support among South Asians in the diaspora. So if you want to be allied with social justice movements, it's important to do that not just here but transnationally, about the scapegoating of minorities and oppressed castes in the subcontinent. And to not fall into

> the trap of supporting a majoritarian project in an ancestral homeland as an extension of your own racial, national, or religious identity here.[85]

She ignores the fact that the pattern of highly educated techies coming to the US and occupying prestigious positions has to do with the US immigration policies based on merit and is not a result of Indian caste privilege. If the US were to give preference to farmers, carpenters or masons, surely many would end up migrating. If the floodgates were opened without restrictions, the diversity of people migrating would be huge.

Subramanian is a major political activist prosecuting the IITs as reproducers of caste privilege. Indians from privileged caste backgrounds have brought caste into the US, she argues, and the recent lawsuits in the US against caste discrimination are just the tip of the iceberg. She writes that,

> ...the vast majority of South Asians in the U.S. come from privileged caste backgrounds, and caste has been a form of capital that they've been able to leverage both in their taking advantage of opportunities for migration and also in achieving certain economic and professional successes in the U.S.[86]

Collaborating with other activists, she has been building a social, political, and legal case against IITians. She has positioned herself as the chief witch hunter determined to demonize the IITs at every forum she can get invited to. But absent from her thesis is any self-awareness that she is helping the Breaking India forces by creating communal violence and divisiveness.

The real question is whether the US Ivy Leagues are a suitable venue to prosecute Indian society, define India's policies, and apply heavy-handed geopolitical pressure. Does the US have the moral authority for making such interventions given its own track record of human rights violations, both domestically as well as internationally? Does the US have any record of success in other parts of the world to solve historical issues of a social nature?

One is reminded of US allegations of human rights violations in the Middle East that led to the deployment of the military. But it was later proved to be motivated by a desire to capture oil. Social scientists have a notorious history of becoming foot soldiers in America's dirty interventions, and the production of atrocity literature by them has been used to justify acts of aggression and conquest in the past.

These fashionable ideas are being imported to India to shatter an already broken education system. The Mittal Institute at Harvard not only supports Subramanian's scholarship, it also conducts seminars to study the role and definition of merit in India. While China forges ahead in raising a generation of top STEM scholars, these Woke ideas are finding fertile ground in India helped by our very own billionaires as well as academicians like Ajantha Subramanian.

Postmodernism has aided the social sciences and humanities to slowly permeate the hard sciences of STEM, bringing in politics, sociology, and anthropology. This is happening worldwide. In Canada, for instance, award-winning scientist and chemistry professor of Indian origin, Patanjali Kambhampati, was refused two federal government grants because he said, 'We will hire the most qualified people based upon their skills and mutual interests.' The Natural Sciences and Engineering Research Council of Canada turned down his $450,000 grant application because 'the Equity, Diversity and Inclusion considerations in the application were deemed insufficient'. The application was rejected at the bureaucratic level without making it to the stage where other scientists could review his proposal.[87]

We have discussed that caste has become equated with American-style racism, databases are being compiled to highlight caste prejudice by Indians in the US, legal action is alleging caste abuses in American workplaces, and the IITs are being attacked as racist organizations. The next chapter examines a key US-based Dalit activist who has integrated all these building blocks and merged the Dalit movement with the Black American movement.

4 | Indian Americans Equated with White Racists

Overview

This chapter details how biased research driven by deep envy against the Indian American community has been causing mayhem in American workplaces where large numbers of employees are of Indian origin. It explains the following:

- A new ecosystem of American activism has emerged that has been collecting data on caste in America – spanning industries, universities, and government – and lobbying to change laws and policies that would result in caste becoming formally recognized as a form of racism under the laws of the US.
- Equality Labs, an organization run by Thenmozhi Soundararajan, is at the heart of a smear campaign against Indians. She uses her Dalit identity and plays the victim card to appeal to the guilt of White Americans. Her organization is not registered as a non-profit because that would subject it to disclosing its sources and uses of funds transparently to the public.
- Its flagship product is a single report on caste in the American workplace. The methodology used was full of glaring problems. At least two other reports on the same subject by well-established research organizations have disagreed with its findings.
- Equality Labs has scored significant legal and policy victories using US laws on racism to file charges of caste bias. Its actions will have devastating consequences for Indian Americans and

Hindus everywhere, as well as the institutional structures of the US, India, and worldwide.

- There is a systematic incubation of Dalit leadership underway in Western universities and Leftist organizations that is then exported back to India. Harvard University is the main hub where this is being done. This US-centric ecosystem has its tentacles deep into Indian institutions.
- Equality Labs has gathered a coalition of US-based organizations that share a common anti-India posture. It has used sensationalism and a well-coordinated campaign to become positioned as the authority on caste for American organizations. It demands employers to conduct caste censuses of Indian employees as a step towards dismantling casteism in their employees. Such censuses and training workshops for management have become a major source of income for Equality Labs.
- Equality Labs, it seems, assumes every Indian and Hindu is guilty of casteism unless proven otherwise. There is no other national origin or religion that has been singled out and treated likewise in the US.

As mentioned earlier, we are very concerned about any kind of bias, including those based on caste. Whenever there is a legitimate case, it should be addressed through legal means. But we oppose exaggerations, falsifications and reductionist theories of blame, excessive victimhood, divisive approaches, and so on.

Compiling US Databases of Indian American Caste Abuses

The US-based Equality Labs group is self-described as a Dalit 'power-building' organization. It suddenly became well-known after publishing a report alleging widespread caste discrimination in the United States within the South Asian diaspora.[88] Through effective messaging to impact progressive Western audiences, the organization has successfully convinced several governmental, educational, and corporate institutions to accept its views and policy recommendations regarding Indian Americans, especially Hindus. In 2016, it received its first grant and began collecting responses for its marquis survey on caste in the United States.[89]

The founder and chief firebrand of Equality Labs, Thenmozhi Soundararajan, was born in California to a cardiologist father, an immigrant from Tamil Nadu, India.[90] She studied at the University of California, Berkeley, and the University of Southern California, School of Cinematic Arts.[91] She has also been affiliated with the MIT Open Documentary Lab, a project that brings 'storytellers, technologists, and scholars together to explore new documentary forms'. Imitating Black History Month, she has launched Dalit History Month.

Soundararajan's methods include media activism, litigation, and diversity and inclusion-related training courses. Equality Labs' website states that its mission is to use

> community research, political base-building, culture-shifting art, and digital security to end the oppression of caste apartheid, Islamophobia, white supremacy, and religious intolerance. Through these methods, we provide practical tools for communities to make new interventions in longstanding systems of oppression and advocate for themselves.[92]

Its flagship accomplishment that gave Equality Labs considerable political clout was its 2018 report, *Caste in the United States*. This fifty-two-page report immediately generated substantial media coverage in the US, India, and even China. Some of its key claims included the following shocking statistics concerning Dalits living in the US:

- Sixty-seven percent reported unfair treatment in their workplaces
- Twenty percent encountered caste discrimination at a place of business
- Forty percent experienced a romantic rejection based on caste
- Twenty-five percent faced caste-related verbal or physical assault

The reader must note that these surveys and the report pertain to Dalits based in the US and not India. Several issues have been raised about the methodological sloppiness and built-in prejudices that undermine the reliability of the conclusions. For instance:

- The US census has never identified Dalits as a category, so it is impossible to estimate the number of Dalits in the US.
- No distinction was made between unfair treatment at work due to racism from non-Indians and specific caste-based discrimination.
- The survey was distributed by Equality Labs' activists to people they selected and was not representative of the broader Indian

American population. This could be the reason that almost thirty percent of respondents identified as non-heterosexual (further categorized into bisexual, homosexual, pansexual, and queer). These numbers appear statistically skewed.

- Equality Labs eliminated twenty percent of the responses for being 'extreme or illogical' entirely using its own subjective criteria that have never been disclosed transparently.
- It also admitted that there was no scientifically valid statistical sampling. For example, there was no external verification of reported caste affiliation (and no consistently applied methodology for self-identification as one 'caste' or another).[93]

The results of this report must be compared with two other caste-related surveys outside India conducted by well-established institutions. One was on caste in the Indian American community undertaken in 2021 by Carnegie Endowment, in partnership with Johns Hopkins University and University of Pennsylvania. The report stated the following concerning the claims in the Equality Labs findings:

> This study [by Equality Labs] relied on a nonrepresentative snowball sampling method to recruit respondents. ... respondents who did not disclose a caste identity were dropped from the data set. ... the sample does not fully represent the South Asian American population and could skew it in favor of those who have strong views about caste. While the existence of caste discrimination in India is incontrovertible, its precise extent and intensity in the United States can be contested.[94]

The Carnegie Endowment report discovered that the majority of approximately 4.2 million people of Indian descent in the US do not 'personally identify with a caste group of any kind', and that only 1% of Hindus reported belonging to a Dalit or Scheduled Caste (SC) community. Less than five percent of Dalits reported having faced caste-based discrimination. A significant number of those claiming caste-based discrimination said that they faced such discrimination at the hands of non-Indians.[95] All this contradicts and undermines Equality Labs' findings. A Pew Research survey of 2021 found that even in India, eighty-two percent of Indians said that they have not personally faced caste-based discrimination and that 'two-thirds of those who identify with Scheduled Castes or Tribes said there is *not* widespread discrimination against their respective groups.'[96]

> "When asked if there is or is not "a lot of discrimination" against Scheduled Castes, Scheduled Tribes and Other Backward Classes in India, most people say there *is*n't a lot of caste discrimination. Fewer than one-quarter of Indians say they see evidence of widespread discrimination against Scheduled Castes (20%), Scheduled Tribes (19%) or Other Backward Classes (16%)."[97]

The other, far more thorough survey on caste discrimination in UK, was carried out by the National Institute of Economic and Social Research. Their 121-page report stated that 'caste exists in Britain: this is not in dispute' but went on to acknowledge that uncovering the extent of caste discrimination in the UK would require an extensive survey entailing complexities, resources, and timelines beyond the scope of their study.[98] This would be particularly challenging given that the British population has not been segmented by caste and hence data on who belongs to a given caste is simply unavailable.

Despite the obvious flaws, biases, and sweeping nature of its conclusions, the Equality Labs report received extensive mainstream media coverage in *The New York Times, The Washington Post, BBC, NPR, Bloomberg,* and other prominent publications.[99] These media outlets did not care to do any due diligence before supporting the report's findings as the gospel truth. Many public intellectuals, such as Harvard Divinity School's former professor from the Black community, Cornel West, also endorsed the report, without addressing any counter positions on the subject as a scholar must when reviewing peers' work. The media did not bother to invite Hinduism experts to their interviews and discussions.

An Indian American Democrat member of the US Congress, Pramila Jayapal, provided a major boost to Equality Labs. In 2019, she partnered with Equality Labs, South Asian Americans Leading Together, and API Chaya to organize a Congressional briefing on caste.[100] Jayapal along with Ro (Rohit) Khanna, a fellow Democrat member of the US Congress, went on to partner with Equality Labs in 2021 to introduce a resolution commemorating B.R. Ambedkar.[101] We want the world to honor Ambedkar, but this should not get muddled with agenda-driven mediocre reports.

Equality Labs is not registered as a non-profit organization obligated to publicly disclose finances or be subject to the same stringent limitations as imposed on political campaigners in the US. This seems like a clever ploy to keep its financials secret from the public.

But indirect sources confirm strong funding support from Leftist non-profits such as those related to Omidyar Network.[102] It operates as part of a broader coalition of South Asian activist organizations that help amplify its messages. The diagram below shows some of the organizations helping disseminate Equality Labs' propaganda.[103]

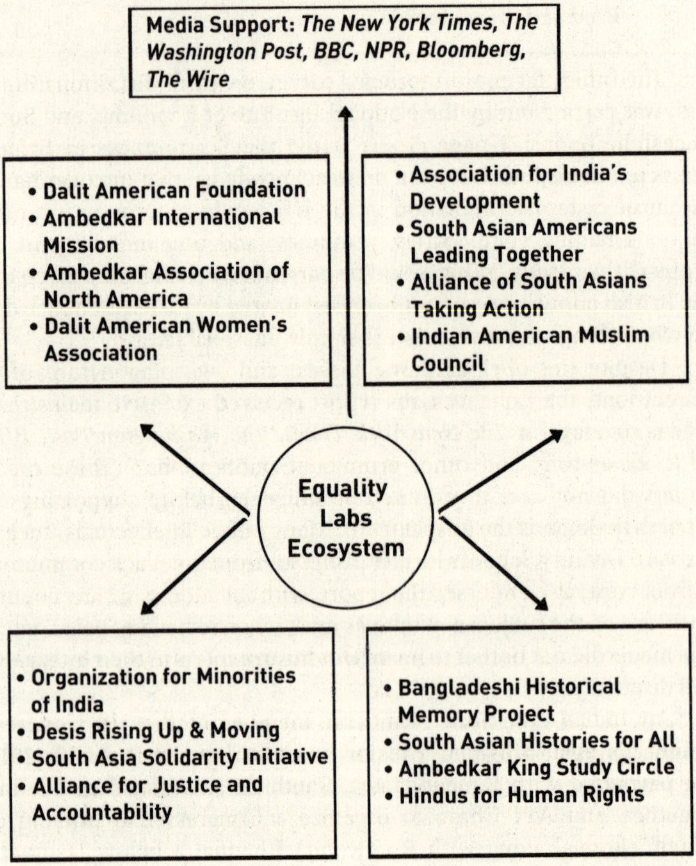

Some of these organizations were also associated with Rutgers University associate professor, Audrey Truschke, and her events such as the *Dismantling Global Hindutva Conference* held in 2021. For her work 'to fight impunity, state violence, anti-blackness, caste apartheid, and religious intolerance', Soundararajan was awarded the 'Atlantic Fellowship' by the renowned Rhodes Trust.[104]

Equality Labs has been particularly successful in garnering support from second generation Indian American social media influencers such as Alok Vaid-Menon and publications such as *Brown Girl Magazine*. An important reason for its success has been the sophisticated quality of its messages, tailored to specific audiences, especially non-Indians. Its views on caste, Hinduism, and the Indian American community are reductive, hateful, erroneous, and even ridiculous. Nevertheless, they are cleverly framed in terms that progressive Americans understand and can relate to, by mapping on to Hinduism and India the familiar tropes and narrative surrounding race in a Western context.

For instance, during a 2018 visit to India, former Twitter chief executive officer, Jack Dorsey posed with a group of women journalists, activists, and writers holding an Equality Labs poster with the phrase 'Smash Brahminical Patriarchy'.[105] Equality Labs' sponsors refer to it in politically correct terms as a mainstream social justice organization at the cutting edge of technology.

Another success factor is Equality Labs' aggressive leadership that is bulldozing ahead by using its alignment with the Black movement. In 2017, as co-founder of South Asian Histories for All, Soundararajan mobilized Black and Dalit activists to testify at the California State Board of Education hearing regarding the portrayal of India and Hinduism in history textbooks. She was reportedly attempting to cut ahead in line, bypassing a few hundred parents and children that had been waiting in line since six-thirty in the morning. California Department of Education security personnel eventually had to remove her and fellow activists for disruptive and aggressive conduct.[106] Soundararajan has characterized such encounters differently, claiming that the California government authorities ejected her four times for 'being Dalit American'.[107]

While Soundararajan paints Hindus as oppressors, the reality is the exact opposite. In July 2022, Rutgers University published a research report titled *Anti-Hindu Disinformation: A Case Study of Hinduphobia on Social Media*[108] proving the dramatic rise and the pervasive nature of Hinduphobia in the form of memes and hate speech in social media. The research used many quantitative methods including (open-source intelligence) collection, machine learning, natural language processing, and time series analysis.[109] And concluded the following:

> We conducted the largest quantitative analysis to our knowledge on the growth of modern day manifestations of online Hinduphobia. Our analysis combines the use of topic expertise and machine learning to deduce underlying anti-Hindu tropes. The analysis shows a systemic structure of consistent themes ranging from exotiscizations, barbarism and heresy, as well genocidal and tyrannical evil. We found that demeaning Hinduphobic themes were often depicted alongside elevated depictions of in-group supremacy

> among the memes of the extremist groups disseminating them. Proliferating exponentially in the digital age, Hinduphobia appears to be reaching new audiences and fueling the group supremacy and feelings of ethnic superiority across the ideological and extremist religious spectrums. These large surges in ethnic antagonism online often presage violence against the targeted groups. Given recent inflammation of ethnic tensions, 34 web platforms, and actors in both government and civil society need to be especially alert for surging coded slurs and imagery associated with Hinduphobia.[110]

Litigations on Caste in the United States of America

There are three main areas in the US in which the research and lobbying activities of Equality Labs and its affiliates have started making shock waves: corporates, university and college campuses, and local governments. These will be illustrated with prominent examples as indicated in the following diagram.

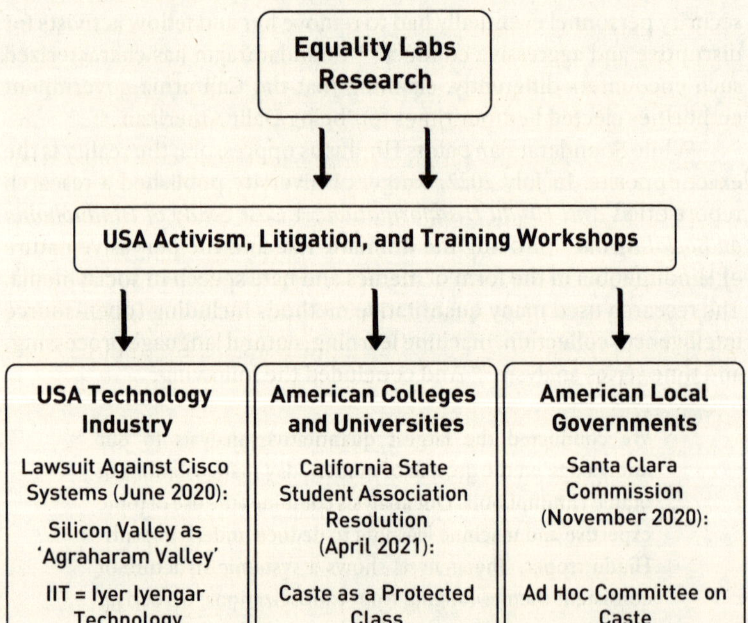

The US Technology Industry

The 2018 report by Equality Labs laid the groundwork for litigation targeting Indian and Hindu Americans, particularly in California. In June 2020, the California Department of Fair Employment and Housing filed a lawsuit against Cisco Systems for alleged caste discrimination on behalf of an anonymous 'Indian Dalit'. The agency claimed Cisco was over-represented by a 'South Asian Indian' workforce and neglected to protect the rights of Dalit employees that are 'the darkest complexion of castes' from facing discrimination and harassment from colleagues enforcing a 'strict Hindu religious and social hierarchy'. The complaint stated that Cisco had failed to prevent 'inequalities associated with caste status, ritual purity, and social exclusion' from its workplace.[111]

The supporting evidence for this was provided by Equality Labs. It further accused Cisco that its caste abusers came from the IITs, which according to Soundararajan, is 'notorious for casteist thinking and processes and policies'.[112] It complained that:

> Upper caste students and faculty that create that very hostile cultures in those academic institutions (like IITs), then go on to create casteist alumni networks in Silicon Valley tech companies. These companies often hire through a process called "internal referrals" ... it's basically caste networking, ... [which] often feed in same folks in same castes, so you have entire departments of multiple companies that are often made up of ONLY upper caste managers.[113]

Hence, Soundararajan wants to make companies 'caste competent'. She sees the Cisco case as having global consequences and feels that it will have an even bigger impact in India than in the US.

Cisco responded that it investigated the matter thoroughly and found no evidence of any caste-based discrimination. Though Cisco is defending itself, its vice president of human resources started to appease critics in a public post:

> While caste is most frequently used to refer to distinctions in Indian society, the concept is a useful one for understanding many different kinds of discrimination based on hereditary characteristics. Isabel Wilkerson, whose *Warmth of Other Suns* helped me understand the insidious nature of anti-Black racism in the US, has written a magnificent new book applying the concept to US racism, titled *Caste: The Origin of Our Discontents*.[114]

The Ambedkar International Centre (AIC) sought amicus curiae status in the case, and the Ambedkar King Study Circle and Hindus for Human Rights joined as well. John Rushing, an attorney representing AIC, told *The Wire*:

> Caste is also a form of race and colour discrimination, both of which are outlawed by California. ... All Dalits are South Asian, and in California, discriminating against someone based on race is illegal. ...If the complainant was not South Asian, and belonged to any other race, he would not have been subjected to caste discrimination.[115]

An article in *The Washington Post* accuses upper caste workers in the US of closing ranks and blocking the hiring of low caste workers. Equality Labs is cited as saying that Dalits have been subject to 'slurs and jokes, bullying, discriminatory hiring practices, bias in peer reviews, and sexual harassment' in tech companies including Google, Facebook, Microsoft, and IBM. Each of these companies has denied the charges of caste bias in their hiring or promotion policies.[116]

Two high-profile Indian American academicians from Harvard and New York University took the matter to *The New York Times*. They used the lawsuits against Cisco and BAPS (one of the largest Hindu organizations in the US) to lobby for the criminalization of caste under US law.[117] They said, 'Making caste a protected category is a critical step toward addressing the problem of caste in America'.[118] This means giving caste the same legal status as racism under the law.

Another article alleges: 'Students from Dalit and other marginalized castes routinely face comments about the color of one's skin, clothes one wears, and general ridicule even over surnames, often seen as classic markers of one's caste identity'. It cites a report by Equality Labs that low caste students face 'micro-aggressions' on American campuses. Equality Labs refers to Silicon Valley as 'Agraharam Valley' (Agraharam being an ancient farm grant given by royalty for Brahmins to practice their traditions). They have nicknamed the IITs as 'Iyer Iyengar Technology', Iyer and Iyengar being common Brahmin names.[119]

This level of media coverage is very unusual given the large numbers of employment discrimination cases filed every day across the US that do not receive similar, or any, attention. Equality Labs has become a catalyst for igniting conversations around caste in the tech world putting Indians and Hindus on the defensive. Such media activism also aims to lobby for caste-based quotas for H-1B work visas to US, replacing merit as the criteria.

We do not deny that there may well be individual instances of caste-based discrimination that take place in the American workplace. They can, and should be, redressed through the laws and corporate policies that are already broadly encompassing. The problem with Equality Labs' proposal is that caste would become the only protected category that singles out as the oppressor one specific religion (Hinduism), one country (India) and one racial group (Indian Americans). For example, other protected categories like race, gender, sexual orientation, etc., are agnostic as to who may be the perpetrator and who may be the victim (e.g., a woman can sexually harass a man). Here, Hindus and Indians are being singled out as the only category of oppressor. This demonizes one particular class of people unlike all the other categories. For instance, there is no equivalent protected category of 'infidel' with Islam designated as the oppressor.

Moreover, in an environment where it is inappropriate and illegal to require people to disclose their racial, sexual, religious and other affiliations, it would not be appropriate to require disclosure of caste affiliations (especially when most Hindus in America do not identify themselves with any caste) in order to monitor caste-based discrimination. What if a Brahmin woman marries one from a lower caste or a White person? In traditional Hinduism, birth caste has been changed to that of their spouse; will corporate policies around caste-based discrimination support this?

The media machinery of Equality Labs and its affiliated activists have begun using the Cisco lawsuit to pressure other Silicon Valley tech employers. Its messaging is that Cisco is guilty of hiring significant numbers of employees from upper caste Indian Hindu backgrounds that adhere to a regressive and rigid Hindu social hierarchy. Cisco should have been aware that caste discrimination would exist among such a workforce, and ought to have offered anti-caste training and included caste in its corporate human resources policies.

Ajantha Subramanian has been called to opine on the Cisco caste discrimination case. Backing the Cisco case, Subramanian points out how IITians have brought caste to America, 'The Cisco case is a threat because it makes the diaspora Indians less secure,'[120] she says, and explains why it should become a tipping point:

> The Cisco case ... fits a broader pattern of dominant caste discrimination and oppressed caste marginalization. ... caste continues to operate in the U.S. despite its invisibility to most Americans. Alumni of Indian institutions, like the IITs, have brought their caste prejudices with them into the

> U.S. tech sector where they attempt to once again assert their dominance. By "outing" the Dalit engineer from IIT as a "reserved category" student, his dominant caste bosses expressed their casteist belief that he had gained admission to the IITs illegitimately, that he was intellectually inferior and unworthy of a job at Cisco, and that he needed to be put in his place. Moreover, they acted with a sense of impunity because caste is not legally recognized as a basis of either advantage or disadvantage in the U.S. It is this impunity to discriminate on the basis of caste that the Cisco case promises to end.[121]

She goes on to claim that,

> ...many of the same forms of descent-based discrimination that exist in India – from the practice of untouchability to discrimination in the workplace and in associational life — continue to find expression in the U.S.[122]
>
> The Cisco case holds out the hope that such policies may be applied more broadly within the academic and tech sectors. The addition of caste to U.S. non-discrimination policies will check the sense of impunity enjoyed by dominant castes and enable oppressed caste students and employees to more openly address ... discrimination. But to more comprehensively address caste discrimination, U.S. institutions should go beyond simply recognizing the caste backgrounds of their students or employees and monitoring on-site social interaction.[123]

Companies that hire offshore contractors and vendors often require those third parties to be subject to standard policies and protocols of their home country. Which means that any caste-related policies that are adopted in the US could be imposed on Indian contracting firms and vendors. This would have a momentous impact on Indians and more broadly, on the tech industry.

Subramanian wants the Cisco, and similar cases, to result in a deeper investigation into caste as a phenomenon on par with American racism. Just like race, caste bias is embedded in institutional structures that continue reproducing caste privilege:

> The protected category provides a legal basis to address experiences of discrimination. ... allow for more

> comprehensive data collection on caste as it's not a well understood category ... And this is not going to lead to a sense that South Asians are somehow backwards (sic) or non-modern. The U.S. is a race society. It's ... segmented along all kinds of lines. And caste is yet another of those forms ... And it's not one that is reducible to race or class. It has its own logic and sort of patterns that need to be attended to. ... caste is no more of an embarrassment than race is. These are both forms of descent-based structures of discrimination that are thoroughly modern. There's nothing archaic about either of these categories, when they're not just holdovers from a premodern or a pre-colonial or colonial past. (They) ... are reproduced through everyday forms of affiliation through marriage, schooling, and more.[124]

Equality Labs has put out a call to collect information about instances of caste-based discrimination in several US tech companies creating an intimidating atmosphere to embarrass Indians. This also confuses HR departments because they see two groups of Indians that look the same and have similar sounding names. Corporate staff in diversity and inclusion are also being forced to get involved; they are confused by these heavily charged inaccurate and negative stereotypes. Activists are demanding corporate management take a deep dive to understand caste as an issue of racial prejudice.

Since American industry is uncomfortable dealing with this subject, Equality Labs and its affiliates are offering 'caste competency trainings' to become politically correct and safe from attacks. In other words, its team of activists show up to coach large American corporates, and thereby protect them from being accused of caste discrimination. Equality Labs has thus created a thriving business for itself.

In 2020, US companies promised thirty-five billion dollars toward racial equality efforts.[125] 'Several consultants in the diversity, equity and inclusion field say that summer 2020 was the busiest period of their careers to date'.[126] This was a combination of COVID-19, and protests over the killing of George Floyd. Companies often cut the risk of lawsuits by signaling their stance on diversity. They accomplish it by allocating a budget for Diversity, Equality, Inclusiveness training:

> Dozens of companies and institutions have sought to deflect controversy over embarrassing missteps or revelations of homogeneous boards and workplaces by launching high-profile initiatives or enlisting a person of color for a prominent post.[127]

We have heard from Indians working in the US headquarters of Microsoft, Facebook, and others, that they are required to attend these 'caste sensitivity training' workshops. They find the content to be sensationalized, one-sided, and outright humiliating. But nobody speaks out from fear of being branded 'casteist', 'racist', etc.

The impact of such lawsuits and intimidating tactics is likely to be far-reaching for companies that employ large numbers of Indians. To track and prevent workplace discrimination, the United States Equal Employment Opportunity Commission requires firms with over one hundred employees to submit demographic data on employees' race/ethnicity, sex, job category, and salary.[128] Similar requirements exist at the state level. Once caste is classified as race and explicitly covered under such laws, *companies will be required to conduct a census and officially classify their Indian and Hindu employees by caste.*

The strange fact is that American corporate HR departments, civil rights enforcement agencies, and courts have gone on a frenzy of activities based on a single unverified report. This lack of due diligence should set off alarm bells even for those sympathetic to Equality Labs' agenda.

American Colleges and Universities

Similar to the tech industry, American college and university campuses also have large Indian populations. On some campuses, caste has recently been designated as a 'protected class', a formal term with legal consequences. Under US federal and state laws, a protected class is a group of people with a common characteristic that are legally protected from employment discrimination on the basis of that characteristic. Federal protected classes include race, skin color, religion or creed, national origin or ancestry, sex (including gender, pregnancy, sexual orientation, and gender identity), age, physical or mental disability, and so on.

Activists are lobbying to have caste added to this list. As a consequence, all kinds of US establishments will start compiling data on the castes of their employees, which in practice means profiling those of Indian origin, and report this data to prove that they do not discriminate based on caste. This will of course open the floodgates for 'caste experts' to offer consulting to the establishments.

We have written extensively about Hinduphobia being prevalent in US academia, particularly in South Asian Studies departments. This move, to profile upper caste Indians as oppressors that must feel guilty of their identity, would undermine all the work done over the past quarter century to fight Hinduphobia. Hindu students and faculty would hide their identity or feel apologetic for it, for fear of being targeted as racists.

Brandeis University in Massachusetts has now included caste in its anti-discrimination and harassment policy,[129] as has University of California, Davis.[130] Several other campuses are at various stages of adding caste to their official non-discrimination policies.[131] University authorities are responding to pressure tactics by some student and faculty activists. Presently, caste is under consideration for the California State University system that has twenty-three campuses across the state of California. In April 2021, the California State Student Association unanimously passed a resolution demanding the addition of caste as a protected class, directing the board of trustees to update their policies and provide resources to better their understanding of caste.[132] This was the first resolution of its kind in any state-wide university system. It described caste as a 'structure of oppression that affects over 1 billion people across the world', and stated that the system comprises Brahmins, Kshatriyas, Vaishyas, and Shudras, and those outside the caste system entirely (i.e., Dalits).[133]

The resolution citing the Equality Labs report, and the Cisco case, stated:

> WHEREAS: All of these inequalities associated with caste status have become embedded in all of the major South Asian American institutions and ... American mainstream institutions that have significant South Asian immigrant populations, with some of the caste social locators being last names, whether a family eats meat, whether they own land in their country of origin, who they want to marry or be in romantic relationships with, and whether they are allowed to be out in their place of worship and community;[134]

The resolution also explicitly called for compliance with the mandates of Equality Labs:

> WHEREAS: The addition of caste within the anti-discrimination policy will make Cal Poly and the larger CSUs in compliance with the recommendations of Equality Labs, an international human rights organization;[135]

And concludes:

> THEREFORE BE IT RESOLVED: The addition of caste as a protected category should be paired with caste

> competency trainings during hiring at Cal Poly and the CSU at large.[136]

As with the Cisco case, such wording begs the question of who precisely would adjudicate whether a Hindu's vegetarian diet or marriage to a same caste person shows caste discrimination. Would Indian origin students and faculty be justified to complain against a university imposing the mandates of Equality Labs so blatantly, and using its 'training' to formulate its policies? Is it discriminatory on part of university administrators with little background on the complexities of caste to explicitly target Hindus?

American Local Governments

Caste has also made a sudden entry into politics at the county level of governments in the US. For instance, a proposal was submitted to Santa Clara County in the heart of Silicon Valley. This is where many of the tech giants that employ large numbers of Indian-origin workers are located.[137] Hence, it is a high-profile jurisdiction selected to maximize the sensationalism.

According to public records, Soundararajan met with the Santa Clara County Commission in November 2020 and convinced them to unanimously approve setting up an ad hoc committee:[138]

> Thenmozhi Soundararajan, Equality Labs, provided information relating to the historical background of caste systems, caste system hierarchy, and caste systems in the modern world. (and) ... relating to widespread caste discrimination in South Asia and the United States. Ms. Soundararajan recounted acts of caste discrimination in the workplace, education institutions, and everyday life.
>
> Chairperson Boren expressed appreciation to Ms. Soundararajan for bringing awareness to this issue. In response to an inquiry from Commissioner Chaykin, Ms. Soundararajan stated that the mission of Equality Labs is to establish caste as protected category, not the caste system to be a protected category, and expressed interest in a public forum to address the issues and provide a platform to the public to share their stories.[139]

A review began on whether to formally pursue caste as an issue, paving the way for policies to track and prevent caste discrimination. The local Indian community also got involved and participated in a public forum where invited 'experts' expressed their views to help inform the commission's decision.[140]

While ostensibly the ad hoc committee was an impartial volunteer body, its vice chairman, Justin Boren, associate professor of communication at Santa Clara University, tweeted a link on the public meeting in which he tagged the accounts of Equality Labs, Dalit Women Fight, Congressman Ro Khanna, Ash Kalra, and Rob (Robert Andres) Bonta (California attorney general). Khanna and Kalra are both well-known supporters of the Left-wing of the Democratic Party and Senator Bernie Sanders. Nobody representing an alternative perspective was included.

During the public hearing, Vice Chairman Boren and Chairman Bryan Franzen repeatedly interrupted representatives of Hindu organizations. They cut off a Dalit representing himself as a proud Hindu on the grounds that his criticism of Equality Labs was tantamount to 'attacking' it. On the other hand, the commission granted Equality Labs considerable latitude, and even allowed someone claiming to 'have caste privilege' with an insider perspective to lash out at upper caste people as being 'violently oppressive' towards lower castes.[141]

Among the 'experts' invited were several anonymous individuals, including one described as 'an expert on H-1B and caste'; another identified merely as a 'Pakistani Dalit professor'; and yet another who was a self-described 'Dalit Queer Non-Binary'. Ajantha Subramanian, professor of anthropology at Harvard was also an invited speaker. She justified the anonymity of these 'experts', saying that 'the number of Dalits testifying anonymously at this very forum attest to the fact that the stigma of caste and the fear of exposure has followed them to the US'. Subramanian advocated for systemic data collection on caste in the US because it could be used to compel academic and technology sectors to set up 'institutional mechanisms' addressing caste discrimination. Her work at Harvard is discussed in the next chapter, and her extreme bias comes out loud and clear.

Equality Labs and related organizations mobilized a considerable number of persons to testify in their favor, including multiple second-generation Indian Americans apologizing for being 'caste-privileged' and condemning the alleged rampant casteism, anti-Blackness, Islamophobia, and gaslighting within their families and communities. Several non-South Asians also testified in favor of Equality Labs.

The Ambedkar King Study Circle issued the following press release following the first session:

> Some of the sharpest commentary came from a speaker who argued that just as she, a white American woman, was in no position to define or refute non-white peoples' experiences of racism, members of dominant castes were in no position to deny that casteist discrimination exists. Her comment was clearly a response to the multiple dominant-caste speakers who repeatedly accused Dalit and Bahujan speakers of fabricating their stories.[142]

Members of the public waiting to testify exceeded the commission's expectations and the session lasted almost eight hours. A second meeting was held during which the commission deferred taking a final decision on whether to pursue caste in its work plan. Chairman Franzen admitted that the issue was far more complex than he had originally assumed. Nevertheless, documentation of the proceedings on the Santa Clara County website still relies on materials provided by Equality Labs and its allies. There are also numerous letters sent by members of the Hindu American community.

A particularly notable document listed on the commission's website is a resolution passed by the National Association for the Advancement of Colored People (NAACP), one of the oldest and most respected civil rights organizations in the United States. It starts with the mention of Rev. Martin Luther King Jr. identifying himself as an 'untouchable'.

The resolution's following allegations against Hindu groups are unsubstantiated and particularly harsh:

> WHEREAS any criticism of caste is lamented as attack on Hinduism by the Hindutva groups. In the Cisco caste discrimination lawsuit, a Hindutva group filed a motion in the California Supreme Court that allegation of caste discrimination is an intervention by the Department of Fair Employment and Housing in Hindu's religious liberty and rights. In California textbook issue the Hindu right-wing groups mobilized 1000s of people including the children to deny the practice of caste in the USA; and
>
> WHEREAS the practice of caste in the workplace is an extension of practice of caste by the South Asians in their day-to-day life; with privileged castes in the hiring-and-firing positions in big corporates, control the social and cultural

> organizations through money power and social networks and access to public offices; left the Dalits more vulnerable.[143]

Such an official resolution, passed by the powerful NAACP and used in legal proceedings across the US is potentially dangerous for Hindus in America. More specifically, Hinduism and 'Hindutva' are being explicitly targeted as the culprits behind this purported discrimination. This is tantamount to ascribing slavery and apartheid to Christianity and monitoring one's adherence to Christian tradition as a metric for determining how racist they are. No one would dare that with any other major religious tradition in the world, except for Hinduism.

Issues and Challenges

Equality Labs is playing the lead role in all the legal cases and proposals/resolutions. It is using its strong presence among students and scholars to promote theories of a rigid caste system, the culprit of which is Hindu dharma. Its allegations claim caste as a Hindu doctrinal practice of a criminal kind. The low castes are said to be dark-skinned and upper castes as light-skinned as a way to play into the emotions of America's Black/White race politics.

Media coverage in all cases across the board has the same narrative and it is the same experts that are paraded from one interview to another. This amounts to branding the entire Indian American community as racists that deserve to be attacked by the ultra-Left Woke movement. Corporations and campuses are being pressured to become suspicious of Indians as a liability. This could impact their hiring and professional advancement and make them insecure in their inter-personal dynamics in the workplace.

All these cases are premised on defining Hinduism as inherently bigoted and oppressive. But the American Constitution prohibits an organ of the state to delve into questions of religious doctrine, and the government does not have the right to define what a person's religion is. Besides, every citizen has the right to know his/her rights and responsibilities, and any notice about violations must clearly point out how the law is being violated. Such laws and their enforcement cannot be subjective, arbitrary, based on hearsay, and so on. The fact is that if one asks a random panel of Indians what the meaning of caste is, varying answers will come forth. Without a formal, widely accepted definition, how could caste become a cause for litigation? Even if there was consensus on a definition, it would be challenging for corporates or campuses to go about determining what a given individual's caste is.

There is the unsubstantiated presumption that a Hindu of Indian descent is necessarily identifying himself/herself by caste and exercising prejudice as per the theory of caste hierarchy. Would people with Indian sounding names therefore, be required to carry certificates of their caste? If this were done to Hindus, why would the same not apply to other ethnic or minority groups and people of other national origins? There is also the issue that many Hindus do not know anything about their caste, such as those whose ancestors came as indentured laborers to Guyana, Trinidad, Bahamas, etc. Second- and third-generation Hindu immigrants to the US, those born of mixed-race marriages, and those who are White Hindus or Black Hindus – most of them are clueless about their caste.

This opens up challenges of equal protection that is guaranteed under the American Constitution, because these activists want to create a class that will be suspect in the eyes of the law, and also because a special set of policies will be applicable only to them.

Of special concern to Indian Americans are the following issues: In a situation involving workplace discrimination, how might an American corporate human resources executive, judge, or jury harbor preconceived prejudice? Would businesses ask employees of Indian origin to list their caste? Would they adopt the Indian government's official caste classifications? Would they assume that a Marathi Brahmin enjoys hegemonic caste privilege over a Telugu Reddy in the same sense as Whites do over Blacks? Would a Gujarati Patel's vegetarian diet be considered evidence of casteism in a discrimination complaint? Would Hindus become subject to blatant hate speech because it becomes tougher for them to defend themselves? Will the bullying of Hindu students being documented in US schools get worse? Will it be justified for Jewish students to demand kosher kitchens in colleges, but considered casteist if Hindu students demand vegetarian food choices?

These must be addressed as American issues under US laws, (even if hypothetically, the Government of India was truly 'fascist') because Hindu Americans have the same right of religious freedom.

Globalizing the Dalit Empowerment Movement

In a 2014 interview, Thenmozhi Soundararajan explained that although she 'came out' as Dalit during her undergraduate studies, it was in the fifth grade she discovered that the Bhopal chemical disaster (a gas leak that occurred at the Bhopal plant of Union Carbide India Limited pesticide plant in 1984) had impacted a group called the Untouchables, which is when her parents told her about her ancestry. In another interview she claimed that Indian Americans in southern California would not allow her to use their main dishware and cutlery at parties hosted in their homes. She says her family had left India to escape caste, and when she publicly announced her Dalit identity, she got blacklisted by upper caste Indian professors and even received death threats.

Soundararajan is being groomed as a leader evidenced by the sheer number of awards she has received.

> Her work has been recognized by the Producers Guild of America Diversity Program, The Museum of Contemporary Art, The Robert Rauschenberg Foundation, Chicken & Egg Foundation, The Annenberg Innovation Center, Slamdance, MIT Center for New Media Studies, The Sorbonne, *The Source* Magazine, *Utne Reader*, The National Center for the Humanities, The National Science Foundation, The Indian Film Festival of Los Angeles and The Alfred P. Sloan Foundation.[144]

Equality Labs describes itself as an Ambedkarite power-building organization, representing both a specific Indian religious and political lens, as well as contemporary American social justice in its messaging and political organizing. Its grassroots agenda involves targeting various expressions of Hindu faith and identity. For example, in a blog titled, *Why Do We Say No To Holi? A Guide To Challenge Casteism*, it excoriated the festival of Holi due to its alleged connections with the 'violent overthrow of an Indigenous king', the murder of Holika (a Dalit), and its marginalization of caste oppression and indigenous peoples' traditions by 'settler colonial' Brahmins. Its call to action was:

> Desist from celebrating it yourself and resist cultural attempts to saffron-wash its violent history.... Share the Bahujan version of the story during dinner. Educate folks about the Brahmanical (sic) control of the history of India, and connect it to the rise of the BJP, Hindu Fascism, and upper caste networks of power. ... Similar to how progressive Americans do not celebrate Thanksgiving to honor Indigenous resistance, think about ways to build power, and support efforts of caste abolition. Share a meal, read Dalit and Bahujan history, and honor leaders who are not from upper caste and Brahmin families.[145]

It has rapidly adopted political mobilization strategies tested in multiple marginalized communities, including those without substantial financial resources. Equality Labs focuses on building a grassroots network of sustainable professional organizations and mobilizing people for direct action in the form of protests, participation in public forums, engaging the media, and crafting legislation.

Within five years, it has successfully reinterpreted the popular narratives of Indian and Hindu Americans being a successful American minority community. The new narrative it has established widely is that the reason for the community's success is the regressive and discriminatory practices they embody due to their religious affiliation. Thus, the new branding is: Wherever Indians go, they take caste with them.

Equality Labs has generated highly impactful atrocity literature tailored to mainstream donors as well as decision makers in government, academia, and corporations. It has the capacity to run multiple campaigns in parallel that set the public narrative using the media very effectively. The doors of elite media, academia, and top-level policymakers have been thrown open to them. As a result of its orchestrated legal action against BAPS, the Hindu American population, despite its claims of being powerfully positioned in US industry and politics, has been put on the defensive and made to look suspicious in the eyes of the public. We support pursuing justice where crimes have been committed. If, for example, BAPS violated labor laws, it ought to be held accountable. But that should not implicate an entire community just like crimes committed by Muslims, Blacks or Christians in America do not result in such branding of those identities.

The concept of Hinduphobia is also being challenged because Hindus are being stigmatized as perpetrators of criminal hostilities against their oppressed Dalit fellow-Americans. As is clear from the legal cases discussed earlier, the presence of a large Hindu population of well-established individuals makes little difference in officials' and administrators' willingness to support Equality Labs.

Equality Labs' activism is loaded with false allegations. For instance, in 2020, a Dartmouth College student accused three Hindu professors of harassing her for being a Muslim. She also said that 'she believed that Hindus like seeing Muslims being tortured'. Maha Hasan Alshawi further alleged that Prof. Prasad Jayanti was a member of an 'Anti-Muslim organisation named Rashtriya Swayamsevak Sangh (RSS)'. She also claimed that he directed a graduate student to inquire about her religion. As to the report that Respondent Jayanti was a member of an anti-Muslim organization, there was insufficient information to support that allegation.[146]

Unfortunately, there is no comparable Indian grassroots organization in the US constantly carrying out similar activities on behalf of Indian Americans operating across corporates, governments, campuses, and media. It will need to be proactive and continuous, and not just reactive to problems. It will need to be professional according to the highest American standards, and frame issues in American idiom.

A Silver Lining

The work of Equality labs may have a silver lining, after all. Finally, it forces the Hindu to fight for himself or herself because the battle is becoming personal. The battle is entering each Hindu's workplace, home and family, and they can no longer run away from uncomfortable situations like they have been doing to date.

But even more encouraging is the recent shift in what Thenmozhi Soundararajan has said. She has started advocating the use of Buddhist meditation (i.e., Vipassana renamed as mindfulness).[147] She is especially impressed by the work of Ruth King, a Black meditation teacher and author of several books including *Mindful of Race: Transforming Racism from the Inside Out.*[148] This can be a gamechanger, and something everyone involved in the issues should support.

On multiple occasions in this book, we have advocated raising the level of consciousness that comes through the various meditation systems developed in India. Only from a level higher than the ordinary ego, which is what Ruth King calls 'from the inside out', can humanity transcend the horrible boundaries of race and other identities. We hope Thenmozhi Soundararajan is genuinely pursuing the path of raising consciousness and we would welcome collaboration to achieve this for all stakeholders.

5 | Ashoka University and the Shanghai Meritocracy Workshop

Ashoka University is one of the most significant nexuses for what we have characterized as Breaking India forces. It is where key databases on Indians are being collected and analyzed, Breaking India theories are conceptualized and intervention strategies are developed, tested, and perfected. This is where many students are trained in ideological narratives and strategies, and then weaponized. New victim groups are identified and nurtured. Heavily backed by Westerners with vested interests as well as by Indians, it behaves in ways that its role in recolonizing India needs to be examined. We point out a complex network of global connections – of people, infrastructure and institutions in India, which are of concern. We do not wish to adjudicate any legal violation, and the purpose here is to present information that would need to be analyzed further before reaching judgments.

While other liberal arts universities springing up across India are playing a similar role, Ashoka is by far the most prominent. However, this is not how its founders envisaged it. They were a group of well-intentioned, successful IIT/IIM and US-educated entrepreneurs with the desire to build a university along the same lines as top Western universities focusing on liberal arts education. Ironically, most of them had tech backgrounds devoid of an adequate understanding of Western liberal arts and how that differs from Indian traditions. It would appear that they were driven by the glamor of showing off their recently acquired wealth by hobnobbing with the global elites. Once a few big names got the ball rolling, many more wealthy Indians jumped on the bandwagon.

As an example of the kind of scholarship emerging from the Ashoka-Harvard connection, Harvard conducted a workshop in Shanghai, China, to discuss *Merit in China and India*. Many Indian scholars participated including Ashwini Deshpande of Ashoka University (who moved from Delhi School of Economics to Ashoka), Ajantha Subramanian of Harvard, Ashutosh Varshney (ex-Harvard Kennedy fellow), and Devesh Kapur (Madan Lal Sobti Professor at the University of Pennsylvania). The distinction between the Indian and Chinese experts was glaring. While the Chinese spoke proudly of the role meritocracy played in building the greatness and glory of China, the Indian participants tried to discredit meritocracy in India's context with a narrative of shame.

The China experts spoke about how the Chinese examination system based on meritocracy was renowned because it yielded great results that the rest of the world wanted to emulate. They presented papers on their history of meritocracy and described how the selection of bureaucrats by Chinese emperors was purely performance-based. One paper discussed the recent rise of Chinese universities in the global league measured on merit.[149] Another analyzed the 'key education policy and planning documents from the inception of the People's Republic of China up to the present time'. Yet another was on the history of meritocracy in China focusing on the Tang Dynasty.[150]

The Indian side was exactly the opposite. The Indian scholars went to Shanghai to tell the Chinese how unfair meritocracy is in the Indian context, citing caste-based oppression and how it is a systemic oppression of Hindu society. This echoes the work of Ajantha Subramanian analyzed in the previous chapter.

As a universal principle, Ashutosh Varshney (an ex-Harvard fellow), supported merit, saying 'Even if inclusionary principles are applied, those meritorious must be given their due weight.'[151] In academics, he wondered whether merit should mean 'academic performance, or an ability to perform and deliver regardless of academic achievement' and whether academic excellence needs to be supplemented with social intelligence. In the absence of a resolution of these dichotomies, he conceded that academic attainment was the only yardstick for measuring merit.

But then Varshney went on to explain that this general rule doesn't apply to India. He launched the subject of caste in India which he said was a hurdle in achieving true merit. In other words, in India's case, the meritorious don't deserve consideration because historically, caste-based division of labor forced people into professions that didn't reflect their aspirations or capabilities. He said: 'Merit essentially came to mean the reproduction of ascriptive social hierarchies in India, an idea a democracy could ill-afford.'

He then equated caste oppression with racism in America. The division of labor was 'tightly regulated' and enforced with violence: 'If violated, the social order, often legally buttressed, was enforced with violence, quite a bit like the Jim Crow American South after the US civil war.'[152]

He expressed concern with Indian democracy being able to 'handle the problem of the upper caste domination of education and public services'.[153] He remarked: 'Were only the upper castes meritorious?'[154]

Varshney differentiated between inclusion in India's public sector and merit in the private sector: 'Inclusionary projects basically mark the functioning of the public sector, whereas the idea of merit, in principle, has migrated to the private sector.'[155]

Ashwini Deshpande asserted that the private sector discriminates against certain castes:

> There is sufficient evidence to indicate that caste disparities in economic outcomes, ... in occupational attainment are neither mainly a hangover from the past, nor are they mainly a result of educational or skill gaps. Thus, members of SC-ST communities will face worse employment outcomes even if they were similarly qualified as the upper-castes, given discrimination in labour (job) markets.[156]

In line with the principles of Critical Race Theory, Deshpande said that difference in outcomes can only be attributed to an inherently biased system. To prove this, she claimed that 'teachers tended to give scripts marked low-caste and female, lower scores compared to those marked high-caste and male'.[157] She went on to suggest that under the pretext of checking applicants' 'family background', employers exercise caste-based discrimination.

> The fact that the two groups enter the labour market with substantial differences in "ability" or "merit" indicates "pre-market discrimination", which means that there are discriminatory factors at work in early childhood development.[158]

Deshpande believes that merit is not 'neutral, objective characteristic, independent of the standard used to measure it, similar to height or weight or the number of teeth'.[159] She therefore questioned the notion that exam performance indicates merit by raising doubts about the very concept of exams.[160]

Discussing students who enter universities using the quotas reserved for lower castes, she said that their lower performance should be blamed on their psychological trauma for being unable to cope with 'micro-aggressions'. Her final conclusion was:

> "family background", a catch-all phrase designed to capture the intertwined effect of class, caste, parental background and social networks, remains the most crucial indicator of individual merit, making the idea of equality of opportunity or establishment of a level-playing field – basic preconditions of meritocracy – very difficult to achieve.[161]

Both Varshney and Deshpande found merit to be a sham in the Indian context, and proposed reservations in private-sector employment. We are not passing judgment on the merit of lower-caste students but merely presenting the arguments put forward by the cabal of caste-race-gender champions in academia.

We are in favor of an objective evaluation process that allows all students, irrespective of their background, to prove their mettle. We also believe that while affirmative action may be beneficial to remove imbalances for a finite number of years, its benefit deteriorates when continued indefinitely, because of the feeling of entitlement it sows in the youth that leads them to discount the virtues of toil and sweat. Moreover, extended protection to a section of the population actually disempowers it because many skills are lost in the process, and it is rendered incapable of becoming self-sufficient. In Chapter 6 of *Snakes in the Ganga*, we give several examples of India's lower caste groups that have managed to climb up the socio-economic ladder with good leaders and internal efforts. None of these examples are featured at Ashoka's discussions on caste.

Harvard's Ajantha Subramanian presented a paper titled *Merit and Caste* in which she reiterated the thesis in her book we critiqued in the previous chapter. She said that merit 'has come to reference forms of caste distinction that have a much longer social life'. Her presentation centered on the argument that caste is reconstituted in technical science education and meritocracy produces inequality based on privilege.[162]

Finally, there was Devesh Kapur whose topic was *Selection Mechanisms and Meritocracy in a Hierarchical and Unequal Society: Indian Higher Education*. He said that meritocracy simply sounds great and fair, but in the Indian context, it amplifies inequalities because of the caste system. He did not propose any new ideas but simply regurgitated the same old concepts on privilege, inequality, and caste. He said the idea of meritocracy being fair is a myth because it doesn't produce equal outcomes. In fact, 'the high degree of tolerance that democracies have for inequality might, in some part, be due to the legitimizing myth of meritocracy'.[163]

Ashoka University could easily have balanced out the Indian panel by including pro-merit thinkers from IITs, IIMs, The Indus Entrepreneurs, and numerous other institutions that pride themselves on India's meritocracy.

The contrast between Indian and Chinese representations of meritocracy in their respective societies is glaring. The Chinese do not mention social issues like Tibet or the Uyghurs whereas the Indians are obsessed with attacking their country's social abuses.

6 Conversation between Rajiv Malhotra and IIT Madras Faculty

As part of the book tour for *Snakes in the Ganga: Breaking India 2.0* in 2022, the authors visited IIT Madras and addressed the student body. The subject of discussion was the attack on the IITs emanating from Harvard, especially the work being done by Ajantha Subramanian discussed in earlier chapters. Post the lively discussion held in a large auditorium, Rajiv Malhotra invited three professors for a candid on-camera discussion. The three were Professors Devendra Jalihal, Ranjit Kumar Nanda, and Jyotirmaya Tripathy. This footage was edited into a YouTube video that has received a lot of attention.[164]

This chapter presents our summary and commentary on the published video discussion. Since the conversation was free flowing and a transcription would not be suitable for print, we have restructured it into the following topics focusing on the highlights of the discussion:

- Allegation that the IITs were founded as elite places with big budgets
- Theory of caste as Cultural Capital
- Is caste relevant at the IITs?
- Allegation: Focus is on computer science so Brahmins do not dirty their hands
- Anti-meritocracy
- Impact on competitiveness
- Methodological flaws in scholarship

- Issues with social sciences
- Implications of this battle in India and globally
- The IITs are unprepared

Malhotra started out by explaining the nature and intensity of the attack against the IITs emanating from Harvard. Besides Ajantha Subramanian's work, a popular Black American author and journalist (Isabel Wilkerson) has argued that caste equals race. And then there are others with tremendous clout, such as a young, high profile Harvard Kennedy School fellow who has hyphenated Dalits and Blacks into a whole new identity theory. As a result, anytime you are accused of being casteist, you are also by default, a racist. This has huge legal and political ramifications in the United States, and these ramifications are coming through the American multinationals to their subsidiaries in India and influencing all the outsourcing organizations in the Indian technology ecosystem.

Malhotra felt that this should be of concern to the entire IIT community including students, faculty and alumni, as well as India's Ministry of Information and Technology, Ministry of Commerce and Industry, engineering related ministers, the Ministry of Human Resource Development, Ministry of External Affairs, and so forth. It should concern Indian technocrats and industrialists worldwide.

Jalihal and his colleagues discussed the 2015 paper by Ajantha Subramanian that appeared in *Comparative Studies in Society and History*, published by Cambridge University Press. The title of the paper was *Making Merit: The Indian Institutes of Technology and the Social Life of Caste*. She went on to build her thesis further with her book, *The Caste of Merit: Engineering Education in India*, discussed earlier.

Allegation That the IITs Were Founded as Elite Places with Big Budgets

Jalihal responded to Subramanian's criticism that the IITs received special treatment and funding, making them elitist. When India became independent, Indians wanted to modernize, giving disproportionately high amounts of funding to IITs. But he pointed out that Harvard University's endowment of fifty billion dollars is almost eight times the total budget of India's Ministry of Education. And yet, sitting in Harvard, Subramanian says the IITs are privileged because they have access to unlimited funds.

Nanda added that just after Independence, India would not have succeeded in building any decent educational institutions if it had made them all of equal stature and distributed the scarce funds equally. Jawaharlal Nehru had a vision of starting with a few institutions of excellence that would contribute to the rest of society.

Malhotra said that as evidence of the success of the IITs, they are producing graduates that are taking over Silicon Valley, and there are more IIT-produced chief executive officers and top-level people than Harvard has produced in Silicon Valley. Harvard is 350 years old. The IITs are much younger, from a poorer country, and yet able to achieve this despite the history of colonization and all the biases against brown people. So, it could be Harvard's envy: it is envious that India, a developing country, has been able to achieve this and made its presence felt on the world stage by producing world class people that beat Harvard.

Another claim of Subramanian challenged by Jalihal is that upon entering the premises of the IITs, one feels as though one has entered a world far removed from the vicissitudes of Indian social and political life. The IITs are typically set on large, pristine campuses funded by the Central Government at levels much above their competitors. But, Jalihal added that American universities too look very different from American towns. Malhotra cited that Princeton University is like a huge township and so luxurious with the land itself worth many billions of dollars. Similar is the case with Oxford University. The fact is that academic institutions the world over tend to have better premises than their surroundings.

Tripathy added that the IITs were built with generous grants from overseas, and not necessarily with Indian money. Even before Nehru, Bal Gangadhar Tilak wanted institutions like the Massachusetts Institute of Technology in India. Nanda mentioned that excellent institutions similar to the IITs were needed to produce a good number of world class teachers. Most of the National Institutes of Information Technology (NIITs) and other institutes have teachers who hold PhDs from the IITs. This helped create a technology ecosystem and a plethora of technical institutes.

Theory of Caste as Cultural Capital

Subramanian's core idea is that caste is capital: that in the modernizing of India, Brahmins could effectively utilize caste as capital and *then* transform themselves into a casteless group, i.e., a group without explicit caste but with implicit and hidden privileges in the form of capital. Jalihal pointed out a problem with homogenizing all Brahmins into one group because there are several divisions among the Brahmins in India: those who know English and those who do not, those who speak English with a certain accent and are familiar with pop Western culture, and so forth.

In her publications, Subramanian cites French Marxist, Pierre Bourdieu who came up with the theory of culture as capital. She adopts it by replacing 'culture' with Indian 'caste'. Malhotra felt that she was applying Pierre Bourdieu incompletely as she fails to say that if the elitist English accent helps get a job, then that is too is a form of capital. Therefore, one cannot homogenize all Brahmins and say that all of them are enjoying cultural capital. Clearly, there are many Brahmins who do not know English. And then there are non-Brahmins who speak better English with an American accent. Her claim that Brahmins have cultural capital assumes that Brahmins are a homogenous group.

Nanda agreed, saying that there is diversity in every aspect: social, linguistic, and caste. A Brahmin from the state of Odisha will have a different lifestyle, privilege, social ability and skill compared to a Brahmin from Karnataka or Tamil Nadu. Therefore, the claim of homogenization that all Brahmins have privileges does not make sense. All Brahmins or upper caste persons do not have cultural capital. Rural Brahmins may not have such privileges. And among the Brahmins, there are different occupational categories, such as education, farming, and so on. Large numbers of Brahmins are engaged in low paying jobs and so putting them in the privileged basket is wrong.

Jalihal clarified Subramanian's thesis: Brahmins use their caste privileges to modernize quickly and then become casteless. She therefore claims that caste blindness (the posture of ignoring caste) is an outcome of privileges. Once you have caste capital, you can modernize and become caste blind.

Malhotra felt that English as a cultural asset or cultural capital is far more important and difficult to acquire than purchasing some sacred thread or anything symbolic. Yet, Subramanian is focused on symbolism as a form of capital, which is easily acquired; anybody can purchase a symbol, as opposed to the Anglicization, Americanization, and modernization of someone's personality, a far more important form of cultural capital.

Jalihal gave his own example: When he entered IIT, he knew English, but was unfamiliar with the pop Western culture, the hallmark for those that dominated the institute. That requires speaking in a certain way, being familiar with certain books and movies, and trends in vogue. These criteria determine whether you are socially accepted or excluded. Inclusion and exclusion are not caste-based in the IITs.

Nanda expanded the discussion saying that some Indian states are overrepresented in the IITs. Therefore, caste should not be the only criteria to decide whether admissions are representative of the population at large. Some states are good at manufacturing, some at entrepreneurship, others pursue academics. Tripathy felt that geographical regions should be another category of analysis besides caste. Jalihal agreed because India's development and economic progress has been very uneven; some regions have done very well while others have not. So just like English is a category, region too should be a category.

Malhotra illustrated geographical advantages by citing that a farmer from Punjab has an advantage in farming because he learned it as part of his tradition, and growing up, and the state has good water supply. While somebody in Tamil Nadu has an advantage being a fisherman. The Punjabi does not have the skill to fish as a livelihood. One could therefore come up with all kinds of theories of oppression based on advantages some possess as a natural phenomenon. It is better to provide equal opportunities and let the outcomes be based on the effort.

Is Caste Relevant at IITs?

Nanda said that in a classroom, one does not see students sitting based on their caste preference. Do you see students asking each other, what is your caste? Do you see faculty asking the students, what is your caste? Don't you see students intermingling? Nobody knows about the other's caste.

The discussants mentioned that it is not possible to know the caste of a person just by their physical appearance. Caste is not the same as race in America, because there is a clear distinction between Black and White. So, the theory of treating casteism as a form of racism is incorrect. Even one's surname is not a reliable indicator of the person's caste.

An important point made by Nanda was that in cosmopolitan communities, hardly anyone knows the caste of others. Hence, it is better to classify people as those who have greater access to resources and those who have lesser access, rather than use caste as a barometer. Malhotra agreed, saying that today nobody knows the caste of people they are working with. When you order food online and take delivery, or dine at a restaurant, you do not know or care to know the caste of the individuals providing the service.

Subramanian's ideas are obsolete and make good rhetoric at Harvard University because there are guilty Whites who make a good audience for her.

Allegation: Focus is on Computer Science So Brahmins Do Not Dirty Their Hands

Jalihal said that according to Subramanian, the IITs have been producing people based on their caste background, claiming that they are educating Brahmins who do not want to work with their hands. Malhotra elaborated that Subramanian correlates Brahmins being good at computer science with her claim that this field is purely theoretical, and they do not have to literally get their hands dirty. Hence, the IIT emphasis on computer science. Whereas Malhotra believed that it is based on market opportunity. If there were a market opportunity for one kind of engineering, then more people would go for that.

Nanda explained the focus on computer science as a market phenomenon. Unfortunately, at that time, there was not a dominant market for manufacturing jobs. The software boom was taking place, so people moved in that direction. He felt it was ridiculous to say that an upper caste person wouldn't want to dirty his hands; Subramanian has no idea what kind of lab classes are required at the IITs. For all the practical lab classes, one has to get his hands dirty. Every engineering student goes to the lab three to four afternoons a week where they must work with their hands.

Tripathy felt Subramanian lacks the knowledge of an insider. She has no idea of the kind of work students are exposed to, starting from carpentry and so on.

Anti-meritocracy

Tripathy summarized Subramanian's argument that there is no true merit at the IITs. What they call merit is actually caste privilege, and this caste privilege is culturally conditioned and cultivated. Furthermore, the IITs perpetuate this privilege because it is not just a place for engineering and innovation, but also for marginality of low caste people and asymmetry. Hence, the IITs are not democratic, and she maps this on to the idea of India being an incomplete democracy.

Nanda commented that she is offending the principle of merit which is raw intelligence plus individual effort. If somebody is putting in enough effort and has the raw intelligence to get into an institute like IIT, we should appreciate that. And attributing that individual effort to a particular caste or privilege is a crime.

Tripathy agreed with the notion that individual industry must replace this idea of privilege by a community. Jalihal said that

Subramanian is completely against arguments for meritocracy, because that simply means continuing with Brahminical privileges.

Malhotra felt that she is disrespecting students because she is trying to make it seem as if they do not deserve merit. She is claiming that based on merit, the lower caste students are unable to compete. This simply reeks of condescension. Tripathy agreed, remarking that the IITs present an opportunity, and underprivileged students are making their best effort to emerge from their station in life. However, Subramanian as a knowledge producer wants them to stay confined to that situation.

Malhotra said that such scholars want students to be victims because they can then take on the mantle for championing for the victims; they want to create victims that do not exist. If victims exist, they want to make their plight worse and keep them suppressed, because otherwise, if the so-called victims say they are empowered in a merit-based competition, then Subramanian would be out of work.

Tripathy found it interesting that the one who experiences marginality wants to come out of it, while the scholar who is in the business of rescuing victims wants them to remain victims to protect her job. This is the difference between the politics of representation and the politics of experience/presence. For instance, I belong to X category, and I am trying my best to come out of it. I study and work hard, so that my life will become better. Maybe I want to get into politics, or however I want to assert my identity, is up to me. More often than not, in the case of students from the IITs, we see that they want to come out of their situation. The scholar is engaged in the politics of representation, and does not want the student to come out.

Jalihal mentioned that Subramanian concludes it is difficult to make meritocracy commensurate with the ideals of democracy because one does not promote the other in the Indian context. By pitting merit against democracy, she says that if you support merit, then you can't be democratic, at least in the Indian context. But, Jalihal pointed out, she might not say the same thing for Singapore or the US, both of which are meritocratic states.

Impact on Competitiveness

Malhotra said that the attitude of anti-meritocracy will make India less competitive. For example, in the field of sports if you get rid of meritocracy, you will have mediocre people on the team, and the team will become less competitive. This is true of any competitive field, be it is sports, technology, military, or anything else. Anti-meritocracy means loss of competitiveness. And without competitiveness, you lose out in the global market. And hence, Indians will become slaves and live in poverty. It is not that Dalits will rise; everybody will be poor.

To compete in the world market, one has to compete based on the rules of the market, and the market runs on competition. Subramanian probably has no knowledge about team sports, or the military which is a competitive area and one must have the best soldiers; or industry, because every industry survives on competition that requires merit.

It is not only the IITs, but every industry, and every neighborhood vendor who is running some business — big or small. He may not be wealthy, but if he is selling something, he must be competitive. A fruit vendor at the street corner must be competitive. He must have merit in procuring and preserving good quality fruit. He must maintain the right inventory and price his product correctly. That person is running a merit-based enterprise. All the entrepreneurs in India, of all classes and castes, whether it is a taxi driver or any other profession, in order to compete and succeed they must be merit-based.

Therefore, to fight against the principle of merit as something anti-democratic is a vicious attack on the survival of a culture, of a civilization in the modern world. Survival and prosperity require competitiveness in the modern world, and this requires cultivating meritocracy. And Subramanian has no alternative proposal. If meritocracy is dismantled, how does one remain competitive? And if one is not competitive, how do you become prosperous?

Harvard has introduced quotas on Asians for admission into STEM education because they do very well in math, and Harvard claims that this meritocracy is a privilege, which is oppressing the Blacks. There is an on-going case in the US Supreme Court whether they should be allowed this kind of anti-meritocracy policy.

Methodological Flaws in Scholarship

Malhotra pointed out that Subramanian failed to invite a peer review for her work from scholars who are qualified and independent. Nor has Cambridge University Press that published the paper or Harvard University Press that published the book. Independent scholars would make counterclaims that should, as a bare minimum, at least be considered, and the merits debated. There was no peer review by India's HRD ministry even though she is talking about their history, nor by opposing voices at IIT Madras. And she does not cite her sources because Harvard's power structure gives her that privilege. Overall, the scholarship is biased and sloppy, to say the least.

Nanda also found her to be unscientific. Jalihal mentioned that she builds a whole argument by citing the feelings of one student named Karthik who graduated from IIT Madras in 1995, and another student named Nagraj. This is unscientific because one can create such characters and write stories.

Additionally, the IITs attract students, researchers, and faculty from all over India, but Subramanian does not seem to understand this complex demography. She picks out the Tamil Brahmins at IIT Madras which is a subcategory, and cites no statistical data. She discusses one specific professor at IIT Madras without naming him. Citing his opinion without any data to backup, she says that those who enter IIT through the Other Backward Caste (OBC) category are haunted for life that they were admitted through their caste quota. But this was just an individual professor's opinion and one should not include this in an academic paper to prove a point. In general, she doesn't have any data or logical rigor to reach her sweeping conclusions.

Tripathy opined that she could be a victim who has been manipulated. Many research grants are given on the expectation that the scholar will write in a certain way to show a certain type of result. So maybe she is a victim of that vicious cycle of supplying bias because the system expects this of her.

Malhotra said Subramanian is playing the Harvard rat race in which they approve of a brown-skinned person attacking his or her own traditions. If the research has prejudiced assumptions to start with, no empirical evidence (merely citing opinions of various people), and no peer review by opponents, then such research does not befit any Harvard professor, Harvard University Press, or Cambridge University Press.

Issues with Social Sciences

Tripathy criticized anthropology as a discipline obsessed with 'otherness', focusing on studying people who look different, eat different, speak different, and dress different. The discipline depends on identifying differences that they claim are a cause for a group's vulnerability and marginality. This is what some self-reflective anthropologists themselves have said.

He went on to say that Subramanian's category of cultural capital is borrowed incorrectly from Bourdieu's idea of symbolic violence, which she herself is indulging in. Creating otherness and then producing knowledge about those others also constitutes epistemic violence. The people who are written about have no scope to write back or to participate in the knowledge production.

Tripathy went on say that anthropologists look for an ultimate oppressor, someone whose aggression cannot be doubted. For example, in feminist discourse, it is essentially the male or patriarchy. Similarly, for caste discourse, it is the upper caste. But in the ultimate analysis, all kinds of oppression become Brahminical, which makes Brahminical patriarchy the ultimate oppressor. The Brahmin therefore remains the ultimate signifier of oppression for this social sciences knowledge.

Jalihal felt that Subramanian is reproducing the Orientalist scholarship that portrayed India as a hierarchy sanctioned by the *Vedas*, reiterated by the *Bhagavad Gita*, and codified by Manu's Laws. She puts Brahmins at the top of the hierarchy, possessing all the advantages.

Tripathy explained that social scientists writing about the IITs use a vocabulary that most engineers do not understand, and hence they are unable to respond. Malhotra commented that social scientists are essentially talking to each other in their own jargon. This is just like having a techie talk to other techies such that a social scientist would not be able to understand.

Tripathy compared the IITs with liberal arts institutions. The IITs provide a certain type of skill that is not found in liberal arts universities. Contrary to her allegations, it is the liberal arts universities that are money spinning venues. Malhotra added that the liberal arts universities are mirroring Harvard and operate like its branch offices in India. There are places like Krea in the south, Ashoka in the north, Godrej Culture Labs, and Azim Premji University, all private establishments importing liberal arts from Harvard. They charge huge admission and tuition fees.

Therefore, if one wants to talk about elitism, one should talk about the liberal arts of India and see how they are educating the kids of the Indian elites in India, mirroring what Harvard wants them to be. That's what Subramanian as an anthropologist should be studying.

Implications of This Battle in India and Globally

How serious is this attack on the IITs that was incubated a decade ago, allowed to grow and develop into its current state? Jalihal remarked that Ajantha Subramanian's framework is now widespread. In India, and wherever Indians go, this framework is being used to evaluate them, to create categories and differences, and to create fault lines among Indians which did not really exist.

Malhotra said that such debates should take place within the Indian system and one does not need Harvard scholars proposing policies, or the US Congress passing some laws on racism. There should be no reason for the legal action against Cisco. This debate should be for the evolution of thought of Indian people from all communities and should be debated openly. But Harvard controls the academic debate using Cancel Culture.

Jalihal said that Subramanian takes the attack to Silicon Valley, post-2005. 'The defense of upper caste meritocracy against low caste quota has been widespread', she writes. And continues:

> Not just in India, but also in the diaspora. In the United States, the IITs' merit is rarely if ever expressed in terms of caste. It surfaces, however, in the face of perceived threats to their institutional brand posed by the entry of low castes. As the extension of OBC quota to the IITs was being debated in the Indian Parliament, alumni in Silicon Valley organized under the banner of 'Indians for Equality' started online petitions, staged public protests and solidarity campaigns, and wrote letters to the Indian President against reservations. At one such public protest held at Sunnyvale, California, a stone's throw from the head offices of Google, Yahoo, Cisco, and Intel, an IIT alumnus working as a Silicon Valley engineer, commented to an Indian reporter: 'let Arjun Singh', who was the Minister of Education at that time, 'do whatever he wants to, with any education institution in India, but tell him to leave IITs alone'.

And then she builds a story on that and how they are trying to protect their caste privileges. She makes a very dire prediction on the impact of the 2005 reservations on post-graduate trajectories: 'My prediction is that the IITian network of institutions' kinship will increasingly fracture and begin to be tracked along general category and reservations category.' As per this prediction, the group of pan-IITians, maybe in the US, will in the future be fractured.

Jalihal said that this fracture is being invented in the Cisco case, where some activists are accusing some bosses of discriminating on basis of caste. Such a fracture is at least being invented, manufactured.

Malhotra said that a template has been created by such scholars and many others tracked in the book, *Snakes in the Ganga,* to explain where this is coming from. The anti-meritocracy and anti-IIT movements are only a subset of a bigger problem that is going on in America.

A certain set of assumptions about India has been turned into a formal framework. Whenever something untoward happens, it gets analyzed within this framework.

The IITians all over the world are brilliant people but their meritocracy will be challenged because of this. They are being accused of Brahminical privilege. In Silicon Valley, lawsuits are being filed against companies where Indians are working. The demand is that Indian workers' caste must be disclosed, they must carry out surveys on caste, and go through workshops on caste sensitivity, because caste is considered equivalent to American racism.

This is an extremely serious matter. It is not only affecting IIT Madras but all IITians; and then beyond IITians, all engineering and Indian techies. The idea being spread is that Indian technocrats are bringing caste into America. There are articles being written along some predefined lines: Indians that we Americans think are helping us by coming here, in reality, are polluting our society by bringing in racism, because they are all infected with casteism. There are on-going discussions that there should possibly be caste quotas for H-1B visas because of the notion that meritocracy is hiding caste privilege within.

There are human resource departments in companies like Microsoft, Facebook, Google, and so on that are examining proposals activists like Equality Labs are bringing in. They are considering what needs to be done with respect to conducting a caste census, modifying hiring practices, conducting a similar caste census in their subsidiaries, and in the outsourcing organizations in India. The fear is that if you are promoting racism in India and bringing products from racist organizations in India, there are American laws that can be used against such multinationals.

Harvard has already enacted an official policy that casteism is racism. And so have some districts in California where many Silicon Valley companies are based. The problem has expanded considerably, which is the reason why Malhotra wanted to bring to the attention of the IITians that there are consequences beyond the local effects in India.

The students sitting in class today at the IITs are going to face this. When they go out into the job market, there will be a stigma that will put them on the defensive. Such a person will be less ambitious and less courageous, because he will think that if he does too well, if he sticks his neck out, he will be hit back by some competitor on grounds of casteism. His opponents and competitors now have a reliable way to attack him, and he must be careful. This means that the person is not going to be as passionate and aggressive about his merit-based success. This is a very big problem.

Nanda said it is unfortunate that every sad incident is being linked to casteism. Academicians love to have an environment where ideas flow freely. But these kinds of allegations will restrict them. He said that many of his colleagues are trying to be very restrained in their academic activities, which is unfortunate. Also, when the students learn of this problem there will be a division among them. Furthermore, those who graduate from the IITs will go with baggage. It might be said that this person is from IIT Madras, and so must have imbibed this oppressive culture and therefore not the right candidate.

In other words, IIT graduates become suspects without any fault of theirs. Nanda said this stigma will travel in his or her career path. Such a student or his organization will not contribute optimally because his ability to perform will be judged from a caste angle, and not merit. Instead of being recognized, he will be suspected.

The IITs are Unprepared to Face the Challenge

Jalihal shared two incidents in which he felt IIT Madras is a victim. The first was an unfortunate incident in 2019. A young female student who had just joined IIT, committed suicide. This was made to look like the Brahmin teachers of IIT Madras had persecuted her and caused her death. The teachers were traumatized and subjected to a lot of media speculation. The second case was a year ago that dragged on until early 2022. One faculty member accused the entire IIT administration of having Brahminical privileges and oppressing the OBCs. This made the IIT community highly aware of the OBC identity, something many of them were previously unfamiliar with.

He said that, unfortunately, IIT Madras lacked any understanding of what they were facing and there was no organized way of reacting to these incidents. They did not know what they had been hit with. The only thing they could say was an internal investigation would be conducted. Malhotra remarked that this shows a complete lack of *purvapaksha* (studying one's opponent) on the part of IITians.

Tripathy felt that the IIT community had this aura of working on wonderful technology that would speak for itself, and automatically insulate them from such crises. But he believed that the IITs' values like excellence and innovation can also lead to its vulnerability. The community gets defensive when such challenges crop up because it does not have the ammunition to respond. This is an asymmetrical warfare in which the IITians do their engineering and sciences well but are unprepared to respond to such situations. He felt that IITs must now acknowledge this reality that is based on people's perceptions. He sees the IITs as elite institutions based on merit, and not elitist based on privilege.

Jalihal was troubled by the fact that such a biased framework can be used against IIT graduates to stigmatize them forever and cause them to not give their best. This is already happening.

Malhotra concluded by thanking the three professors for their thoughtful rebuttal and giving the perspective of the real stakeholders of the IITs. He promised to continue to serve as the eyes and ears for the IITs looking at such syndromes, and express himself audaciously.

He said that he has taken on a very aggressive, big bully at Harvard. It is the place where these kinds of theories are being churned. He needs moral support from the IITians and even technology people from anywhere in India. All of them have an obligation because they are product of the IITs, which gave them all the success they achieved in their careers. The IITians should stick their necks out to defend their institution, and not be worried about the need to be non-controversial for the sake of the next award, the next deal, or the next committee to join. It is now payback time and give back to these institutions and the culture that they came from.

7 Battle for Higher Education: Social Sciences Versus Hard Sciences

This chapter takes the battle for the IITs into the broader framework of the battle for higher education. Though we limit our scope to higher education, the transformation of higher education flows into an even larger battle: the battle for the future of society.

To forecast the future trends in India's higher education, we must study the present impact of Critical Race Theory in American education, because India has been importing American liberal arts (and hence CRT) at a rapid pace. What happens in American education is being spread worldwide and India is the largest recipient of this influence.

We will discuss two dimensions of this broad transformation in higher education:

- Social justice implemented through programs in Diversity, Equity, Inclusion. The theoretical frameworks are determined by social scientists committed to Critical Race Theory.
- Sustainability programs: These manifest in industry as Environmental, Social, Governance (ESG), and large Western consulting firms are driving these – such as Ernst & Young, Deloitte, PwC, McKinsey, and so on.

These two have become inseparable in recent years. Though sustainability started out referring to the environment only, its scope has expanded into an umbrella framework for human well-being in the broadest sense. Brookings Institution makes this integration clear:

> Sustainability is now understood to extend beyond the environment to incorporate equity, justice, and opportunity, to ensure the long-term viability of communities.[165]

Sustainability drives ESG, which is the basis for the corporate social credit system by which corporates are rated and investors choose them according to their ratings. Officials concerned with DEI have entered deep into all organizations including corporate, academic, government, and so forth.

This two-pronged sustainability and DEI thrust is a comprehensive plan that has taken over American K-12 education, higher education and research, and industry. India is now the prime target for what amounts to a recolonization of its institutions across the broad spectrum of society. The overarching framework mandates the integration of environmental protection and social justice in all walks of life: education, business, and government. Most American universities are heavily invested in this framework.[166]

Our posture is that we fully support the stated intentions behind DEI and sustainability movements. But as we explained in the book *Snakes in the Ganga,* in practice these ideologies suffer from several issues: They undermine meritocracy, replace individual rights with identity politics, worsen the divisiveness among groups, and thwart academic freedom and free speech by adopting Cancel Culture. In general, this lowers the standard of education and research.

It is also important to note that dharma is fundamentally a path of sustainability. But as interpreted in Western discourse, sustainability is being defined from a perspective of Western Universalism (WU). This raises fundamental questions on whose values determine the criteria and goals for sustainability. Vedic metaphysics states that nature is a being with her own rights. But Western Universalism states that nature is humanity's property and damage to it is a loss of human property, and hence, bad for industry and consumerism. Vedic ideas are thus considerably different from Western ideas of sustainability. The core principles of dharma like *ahimsa* (non-violence), vegetarianism, animal rights are not given adequate weightage in Western Universalism. The rubric of ESG and therefore sustainability is biased and should not be blindly adopted by Indian society. The sustainability model based on Western Universalism also privileges victims based on oppressors and oppressed.

Thus, a foundational debate is this: Who decides the list of victims entitled to become protected classes as the oppressed? Why not include

Hindus as the natives of India who were victims of foreign oppressors for one thousand years? Or the natives of Arabia/Iran/Turkey before the Muslim takeover of those societies? Why are Muslims exempt from being classified as oppressors?

Not only are the frameworks being controlled by Harvard University, US consulting firms, United Nations, World Bank, and other global players, but also the actual measurements of ratings and reporting are controlled by Western companies. India has no say in the matter.

There is a grand architecture being installed in America to Wokeify society in all its dimensions. From cradle to grave, Wokeism has penetrated all institutions. It is now just a matter of time when we realize that education, the workplace, the government and our personal lives have been pierced by this ideology.

The diagram that follows depicts how CRT embedded in social sciences and liberal arts has permeated every major organ of American society pushed by some very powerful entities and individuals. India is only a few years behind.

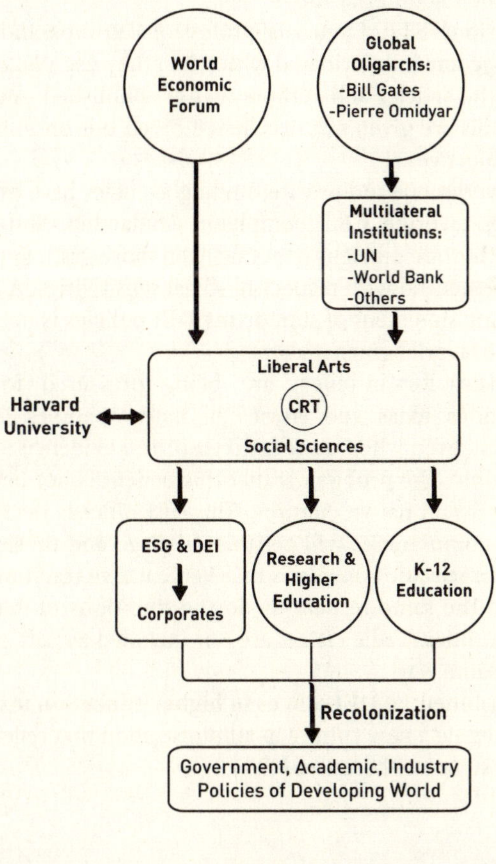

Wokeism Enters Research and Higher Education

In particular, we will look at the following trends in the American STEM higher education:

- **Loss of academic freedom** to pursue science and publish results, because of the demand to be politically correct and sensitive to feelings of vulnerable groups. In other words, what used to be objective scientific pursuits must now be modulated by social sensitivities that are subjective. This lowers the level of rigor in research. Academic research is pushed in directions mandated by DEI or sustainability goals, which is unprecedented.
- **Cancel Culture** in STEM higher education is becoming pervasive as a powerful weapon to silence, fire, and instil fear in academia. This comes from the application of Marxism, that the dominant culture has been oppressing the victims and needs to be silenced in order to give the victims a chance to build their counternarrative.
- Professional STEM journals, professional groups, and societies have become indoctrinated with CRT; they use Woke filters to select the articles and authors that get published. Awards and accolades are given not excellence-based but on fulfilment of DEI objectives.
- US government and private funding agencies have established policies favoring CRT compliant scholarship, and in many cases, they are outright rejecting even those grant applications that are neutral with respect to social sensitivities. A clear and emphatic statement of supporting DEI policies is necessary to win the favor of grant-makers.
- Scientists, for instance, are being pressured to include indigenous ideas and stories of native peoples into their research, even when there is no empirical evidence to support the claims. The problem is that this benefit is not being given equally to all native cultures. The DEI officials decide which native communities will get this privilege and those that will not. Our specific concern is that Vedic native traditions do not receive the same respect as do the traditions of many other communities. Vedic claims are not included as part of science in the same way.
- Establishment of **DEI offices in higher education institutions** are bringing a new culture in administration that reflects a new power structure based on CRT.

So, it is simply a matter of time before these disastrous practices are brought into India to destroy the institutions of excellence that have been built post-Independence.

Academics have always valued freedom. We can safely say that academic freedom to pursue knowledge is the primary reason many of them sacrifice the benefits of business careers. They have been able to follow their interests and direct their research without restrictions or boundaries. This freedom is at risk because sociologists are being placed at the helm to direct STEM research projects even though sociologists are unqualified to judge the merits of STEM research. In the guise of inter-disciplinary and trans-disciplinary research, activist professors from the humanities and social sciences are controlling what STEM scientists should study. They are mandating that the problems be selected and investigated through a social sciences and liberal arts lens, a lens that is impregnated with CRT.

Social Scientists Become the Sustainability Police

Social scientists have consistently been envious of the hard sciences and wanted to rein-in STEM research. But they failed to do so in the past. Unfortunately, this is all about to change. We are seeing two parallel, but intercoupled, developments emerging in universities:

- **One is the spread of DEI officials and administrators. Yale University, for instance, is reported to have as many administrators as undergraduate students as of 2021,** and there are more administrators than faculty members.[167]
- The other trend is the establishment of SDG offices in leading universities.[168] These SDG officials are also beginning to boss around like the big brothers looking over the shoulders of researchers dictating to them the kind of research they should pursue.

Stefania Giannini, UNESCO's assistant director-general for education said in a global forum SDG conference that 'There is a strong social justice imperative here', referring to universities.[169] She wants higher education institutions to move to democratic values and civic engagement as part of their social responsibility. She stressed moving to a 'trans-disciplinary approach' that connect hard sciences with the humanities and the adoption of a diversity-based model.

The United Nations has a strategic plan to push forward these social sciences models and use them to meddle with the hard sciences. This is being thrust worldwide through all its agencies in the name of interdisciplinary and transdisciplinary collaboration to solve the 'wicked problems' facing humanity. The UN believes that,

> interdisciplinary synergies are needed on the one hand, such as those between STEM and the social sciences and humanities (SSH). And on the other hand, transdisciplinary cooperation and partnerships with non-academic partners such as policy makers, civil society actors and industry. Inter- and transdisciplinary approaches to the SDGs are fundamental in promoting the capacity to understand and act on 'wicked' problems and are essential to align education outcomes with the SDGs.[170]

Such social sciences demands are, in turn, controlled by CRT scholars perched in powerful places like Harvard. In effect, this weaponizes the UN into a Woke machine.

On top of this, global elites like Bill Gates along with the World Economic Forum (WEF) are controlling the UN apparatus in order to change how universities are to be organized, the kind of work they must embark on, and the kind of research they can publish. The global elites, the WEF and the UN are busy trying to redirect the output of STEM researchers.[171]

The UN is clear that it wants Higher Education Institutions (HEIs) to 'restructure their strategy and integrate sustainable development in their systems in a holistic way to respond to the current societal challenges'. This is important because,

> HEIs are in a unique position in society as they are considered neutral and influential players, which allows them to foster dialogue. Their position stimulates and encourages interdisciplinary collaborations by bringing together expertise from various fields such as social sciences and humanities (SSH); science, technology, engineering and mathematics (STEM); medical sciences, and other related domains.[172]

Columbia University began a new initiative several years ago initially to address climate change problems, under the banner of Columbia World Projects, which was 'a university-wide effort to experiment with how to institutionalize this ambition of uniting academic capacities with agents of change, all in service to the public good'.[173] However, this scope expanded rapidly to include a much broader definition of the 'service of the public good'.

The open question never adequately explored has been: Who decides what is in the best interests of humanity at large, and by what criteria? The even bigger question is who signed up for this new world order?

Woke activists are on a mission to force the acceptance of social scientists to lead the hard sciences in the name of interdisciplinary research. A powerful weapon controlled by social scientists comprise toolkits by which STEM research and education as well as corporates are to be scored and rated.

For example, in the case of universities, social scientists have been developing scoring methods like the 'Interdisciplinarity Sustainability Index' a social credit system for STEM researchers to measure their collaborations. The following statement of this intervention summarizes how social sciences theories are being turned into indexes for use by 'university managers' (i.e., DEI administrators aligned with Woke):

> Utilising a quantitative text analysis, we examined a database containing over 30,000 entries representing the university's SDG-related scientific production from 2015 to 2019. ... we conducted a social network analysis (SNA) of co-authorship to measure interdisciplinarity for each SDG. We defined interdisciplinarity as collaboration among researchers in diverse disciplines. We employed a modularity algorithm to select bottom-up clusters of researchers from diverse departments. Finally, we analysed the identified clusters to propose an Interdisciplinarity Sustainability Index (ISI) capable of identifying the most investigated and interdisciplinary SDGs. ... our results enable the quantification of interdisciplinary SDG research via the proposed methodology. The study helps to visualise inter-departmental collaborations and thus informs university managers' efforts to identify and coordinate compatible research groups to bridge inter-organisational boundaries.'[174]

Besides controlling STEM researchers, there is also a push to use STEM students. The stated goal is summarized as follows: 'To prepare STEM students to become potential change agents, they must learn to apply their theoretical knowledge to the three pillars of sustainability: economic, environmental, and social'.[175]

These rubrics to measure social credit are already running into problems with the corporates' self-appointment as moral police, as seen in the recent pushback against ESG. Many experts disagree on the assignment of scores, such as the following critic:

> Take the case of Pepsi and Coca Cola. Both companies get high ESG scores from the biggest ratings firms. They are also typically amongst the largest holdings for ESG funds, largely because they rank high on parameters such as corporate governance and greenhouse gas emissions. ... their core businesses involve the manufacturing and marketing of addictive products that are a major cause of diabetes, obesity, and early mortality. Pepsi and Coke leverage their power to prevent taxes and regulation on their businesses and fund large amounts of research to divert attention away from the health impact of their products. With the cost of diabetes now over $300 billion annually in the United States alone, the human and economic harm caused by these companies may outweigh their economic contribution.
>
> Technology companies such as Alphabet, Amazon, and Facebook also tend to be among the largest holdings for ESG funds. They often get high ESG ratings because they are predictably low producers of greenhouse gas emissions. But few would consider them to be good corporate citizens. Amazon has deplorable labor practices and engages in predatory pricing. The business models of Facebook and Alphabet involve algorithms that have made dangerous hate speech and misinformation ubiquitous across the internet, and the companies' products have been tied to an increase in mental health issues in young people. All three firms have been labelled by academics, policymakers, business leaders, and attorneys general as monopolies that threaten the existence of a well-functioning free-market system. If a company's core business model does so much harm, the cover-up through "good behaviour" on other parameters shouldn't be so easy.[176]

The recent bankruptcy case of FTX Trading Ltd. also illustrates how philanthropy and the fashion of impact investing are being used as a camouflage to cover up abuses. Another kind of bias in ESG is illustrated by the way Elon Musk suddenly fell out of favor with many on the Left, and then Tesla, his electric car company received poor ratings from the ESG police.

Pushback in American Academia

To examine the threats to academic freedom, in November of 2022, Stanford Business School arranged a conference titled *Academic Freedom Conference*.[177] Heavyweights like billionaire founder of PayPal, Peter Thiel, along with many 'canceled' academics like Jordan Peterson attended the two-day conference to assess Wokeism's takeover of academia including STEM education and research, and to discuss the way forward. The conference was supported by many Ivy League alumni associations, including Cornell and Harvard Alumni for Free Speech, that are against the prevailing Woke Cancel Culture pervading their alma maters and other prestigious American universities.

Researchers of STEM have been busy with their heads buried in their research while the Woke mob has slowly entered STEM HEIs in the US and taken over the reins of STEM departments. The *Chronicle of Higher Education* declared the Stanford conference to be 'a threat to democracy' and many administrators at Stanford demanded that this conference to discuss the state of academic freedom should itself be canceled.

John Cochrane of Hoover Institution observed that there were three different types of blocking of academic freedom under way: direct action by the institution; individual self-censorship; and blocking by funding agencies and academic journals.[178] This shaming, ostracizing, defunding and ostracizing is the result of CRT's built-in tool of Cancel Culture.

Jonathan Haidt, social psychologist at New York University spoke about why universities in the US and the UK had changed radically since 2014-16. He attributed it to the huge increase in serious mental health among Gen-Z (those born between mid- to late 1990s and the early 2010s), especially girls. He said that universities were set up with the mindset and institutional structures for the pursuit of truth. But in 2014, the new Gen-Z entered colleges with demands for social justice replacing the quest for truth. The goal or the telos of the university changed from truth seeking to social justice. Haidt goes on to say that the joy of research was replaced by fear, anger, identity demands. The social justice rhetoric drove out the moderate middle and turned the campus into individuals on the extreme Left and extreme Right fighting each other. Previously compartmentalized departments like Grievance Studies, and so on suddenly got interconnected with each other by social media to create a giant Woke ecosystem.[179]

Some scholars at the conference predicted that existing prestigious institutions like Stanford were so badly infected with Wokeism that they could not be resurrected. Scholars from Hoover Institution, which is a conservative bubble within Stanford, discussed some of the shocking revelations that show the direction in which research in the hard sciences was heading. Many examples were cited to show that the DEI offices in American universities are acting like commissars dictating the kind of research that is allowed, and even stripping top scientists of academic freedom in their fields of expertise.

One scholar complained about the politicization of academic research:

> You would think that this lack of academic freedom is mostly in the humanities, social sciences political discussions but they are also infecting hard science now in a big, big way. Not just the DEI bureaucracy, I think we're all for a diversity equity and inclusion. But this is not about that. This is about political litmus tests, which is very reminiscent of what the Soviet Union required in its purges.
>
> The number one thing you have to do in a DEI statement is to show the depth of your knowledge and your capacity to talk about DEI. And pledge how you're going to work with the DEI office in the future. This is a political test... The journals, and professional societies have both policies and constant political editorials. The one that shook me most is what already exists in Stanford as the institutional review offices which are expanding (in scope), where before you do research, you must submit to an institutional review of the social consequences of (your) research and how it might hurt marginalised populations; to the point that what might diminish employment can't be published. Sorry Mr. what about that steam engine but you know it might have effects on the marginalised coal miners. Things that are potentially dual use technology won't be funded anymore or you won't be allowed to publish these things anymore.
>
> This isn't quite in place yet but that is what is coming and most striking. So dual use technology - if your chemistry or your laser might be useful for shooting down Chinese

> missiles that are going to Taiwan, sorry we can't find that sort of thing. So that is the politicisation of hard science was the thing that was newest to me and I think was most shocking.[180]

Theoretical physicist, Professor Lawrence Krauss, spoke on *Is Woke Science the Only Science Allowed in Academia?* wherein he gave numerous examples of how the National Science Foundation, the US Department of Energy and other major grant-giving institutions have changed their priority from focusing on science and problem solving to giving grants using the DEI lens. Even those institutions awarding excellence in science research have been hijacked to give awards based on DEI. He offered the following concrete examples showing how DEI has taken control of research:[181]

1. Tomas Hudlicky of Brock University wrote a paper in which he questioned whether efforts to promote diversity by prioritizing inclusion of certain groups could compromise meritocracy. His article was retracted from the journal and the editors of the journal were replaced.
2. Alessandro Strumia, physicist at the University of Pisa, gave a presentation at The European Organization for Nuclear Research's (CERN) first workshop on high energy theory and gender. He tested the hypothesis that there is a gender bias against women within the academic circles of physics. However, his results suggested that male rather than female scientists could also be victims of discrimination. His subsequent seminar on the subject was cancelled by CERN, his slides were removed from the conference website and his position at the lab was revoked. Over four hundred physicists condemned his conclusions in a public statement, not citing flawed data analysis but issues with the outcome from a political perspective.
3. The Department of Earth, Atmospheric and Planetary Sciences (EAPS) at MIT, canceled the prestigious EAPS' John H. Carlson Lecture because the speaker turned out to have expressed a dissenting opinion, on a topic unrelated to about climate science.
4. University of Chicago geophysicist Dorian Abbott argued in a *Newsweek* piece that universities' obsession with Diversity, Equity and Inclusion threatens to derail their primary mission on 'the production and dissemination of knowledge'.
5. The Royal Society of Chemistry has announced a formal policy not to publish any content that could reasonably

offend someone on the basis of their age, gender, race, sexual orientation, religious or political beliefs, marital or parental status, physical features, national origin social status or disability. Regardless of the author's intent, they said that the perception of the recipient is what matters.

6. Even prestigious journals like *Nature* have become Woke. They feel that research should not be evaluated only on the basis of its scientific soundness and merit but avoid supporting findings that seem to discriminate some identity.[182]

Another mandate is to acknowledge and incorporate the native, indigenous and traditional knowledge systems into the hard sciences. Professor Krauss listed many ways in which Western academia was fast becoming woke. He cited the example of Francis Widdowson, an astronomy professor from Mount Royal University, Calgary who posed a question to Dr Gregory Cajete, a professor of Native American studies and education at the University of New Mexico. Cajete discussed the importance of incorporating indigenous peoples' knowledge of the stars into science courses. Professor Widdowson asked how such native star knowledge with respect to astronomy could be incorporated since native peoples did not have a telescope and she questioned the contribution to the courses in hard sciences at Mount Royal. Widdowson was promptly fired from her tenured position for posing questions that made Native Americans feel insecure.[183]

While Woke activists celebrate the rights of native and indigenous peoples' culture, we see that the same acknowledgment and respect is not afforded to Indian knowledge systems. Is it that Indian traditional knowledge systems like Ayurveda and meditation practices pose a genuine threat to Western Universalism? Time and time again, we have seen that only after properly digesting Indian knowledge systems into Western Universalism, the same Indian native traditional knowledge becomes safely domesticated as Western Intellectual Property. Why is there no inquiry into how this practice of digestion, domestication, and repackaging impacts sustainability of Indian native culture?

A biologist pointed out that the differences between males and females are well-established in all animals, both physical and behavioral, and is not caused by human society. Sex is a binary and not a continuum. Yet such established facts of evolutionary biology are being declared false and the differences between genders is deemed to be the result of social conditioning and not biological. The professor explained that genetic differences cannot be denied between ethnic groups or genders. However, research on ethnic differences in genetics are criticized due to the fear of eugenics; on the other side, such research produces benefits for medical uses. The scholars lamented that funding sources are now supporting identity politics rather than science breakthroughs. Social justice considerations are now the main criteria for research funding, basis for promotion, and publishing. Researchers who dissent get demonized, ostracized, and even fired.[184]

Another observation made at this Stanford conference was that even in classes on subjects like chemistry, Wokeism is the new criteria for excellence in teaching. Some professors teach topics like decolonization, anti-racism, and gender identity, and science classes begin with each student introducing their pronouns on the first day of class.[185]

A *Wall Street Journal* report cites the bloated administrative staff at Stanford: 'For 16,937 students, Stanford University lists 2,288 faculty and 15,750 administrative staff',[186] and blames them for implementing social justice initiatives called *The Elimination of Harmful Language Initiative* at Stanford. This is a multi-phase project of Stanford's IT leaders that spent eighteen months to produce a list of words that ought to be eliminated from the campus.[187] Students gave a standing ovation to a speaker saying: we must cast in stone a list of things that can and cannot be said on campus.[188]

In some campuses, bootcamps are being held by DEI officials. Once DEI departments are established within STEM departments, then all student admissions, faculty hiring, and even research direction is controlled by the mandates of the DEI staff. Anyone opposing or even merely questioning these decisions is swiftly dealt with either by extracting an apology or canceling them or even firing them from tenured positions.

Necessity for a Debate in India

In response to Woke, the US has a significant and growing academic pushback as evidenced by the Stanford conference discussed above. Unfortunately, there is no similar initiative or competence in Indian academics despite having a Right-wing leaning government.

Each of the changes we discussed in technical educational institutions in the US is being echoed in India's premier institutions such as IITs and Indian Institutes of Management (IIMs). The UN's Higher Education Sustainability Initiative has already penetrated the IITs and the IIMs:

> It's not just IIM Ahmedabad that has integrated sustainable development into its curriculum. Several leading universities and centres including the Indian Institutes of

> Technology, the University of Madras, Jadhavpur University and TERI University have focused on the importance of education for sustainable development.[189]

The problem is not with supporting sustainability, but with the fact that this is a Western initiated movement channeled through its institutions as well as multilateral institutions under its influence. In India's context, it has to be defined in accordance with Vedic principles. It cannot be some mandate of global elites or the United Nations.

The IITs have laid the first foundational step by establishing the office of Diversity and Inclusion with Woke administrators as heads.

IITs at Risk: Structure, Student, Faculty, Alumni

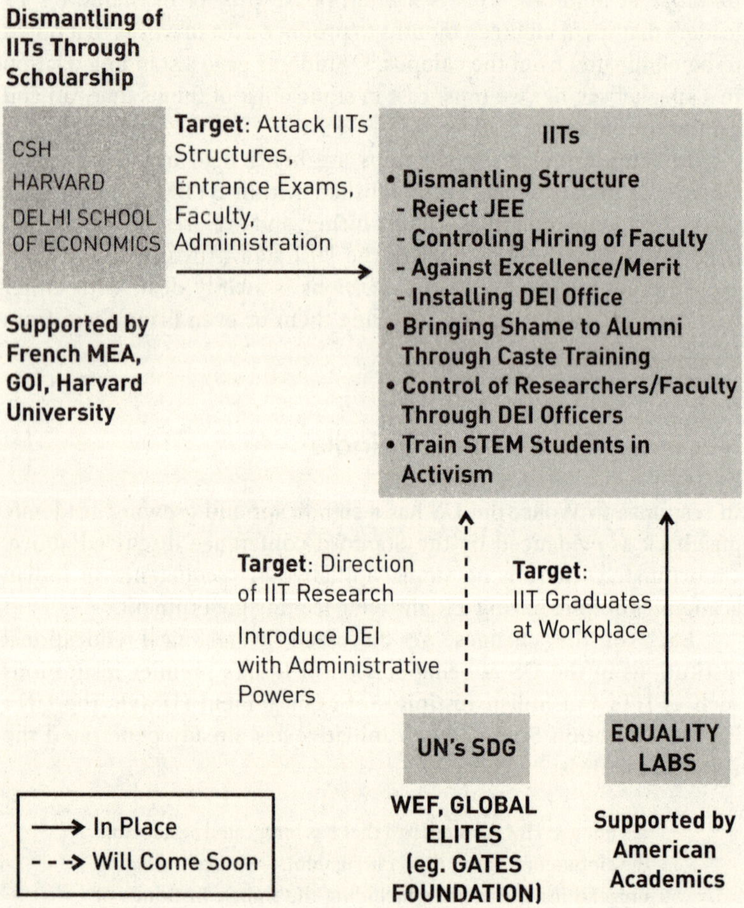

Recently, IIT Madras has proudly announced that it will offer Masters' and PhD programs starting in 2023, as part of its social sciences. The faculties, frameworks and standards, course materials, and direction is coming from foreign (mostly US) institutions that are involved in championing CRT applications to society. All stakeholders of the IITs are at risk – alumni, faculty, current and future students.

India needs to take swift action, not only by refuting the academics that originate and propagate this activism, but also by confronting the problems on the ground. Specifically, the following need to be addressed:

1. Invest heavily in Vedic social sciences, not based on chauvinism or taking pride in the ancient past. The focus should be on addressing present issues using Vedic frameworks.
2. Strengthen the quality of IITs and other educational institutions with a focus on excellence and not identity politics.
3. Review research in existing social sciences departments in India, such as the Delhi School of Economics, and cut funding when this research is contrary to the national interest.
4. Purvapaksha on Wokeism should be done so that scholars, policymakers, bureaucrats and other stakeholders understand Woke history, principles, terminology and toolkits.
5. We pointed out how the French Ministry of External Affairs has funded initiatives in sensitive data gathering and research to dismantle engineering education in India. India should counter such Breaking India initiatives by any foreign agency.
6. The United Nations has become a mouthpiece and apparatus for use by foreign agents, be it China, the World Economic Forum, or global elites with Breaking India agendas. India should investigate how international organizations such as the IMF, World Bank, the United Nations have been hijacked and are vehicles that pressure India with policies that could potentially be against its national interest. These policies are clothed in nice initiatives like sustainability and whole community development, and so on. It is important to follow the money trail and ideology trail to understand the motivations of the funders.
7. Educational institutions should move away from international rankings because these are often based on Woke ideas of holistic education, whatever that means. For example, the UN website on sustainable development openly states that the performance of higher education institutions must be judged on their contributions to the UN's SDG goals, which we should be reminded are the goals of the WEF and other billionaires.[190]

8. Mobilize grassroots activism by families to fight the anti-meritocracy movement.
9. Afflicted with Wokeism, India's chief justice, D.Y. Chandrachud is already questioning the entrance exam criteria for engineering admissions. If left unchallenged, such persons will open the floodgates for Marxist social engineering.

Our message to ALL Indians: You can run, virtue signal, sleep; but you cannot hide. They are coming for you!

Endnotes

1. See: 'IIT-D to set up office to 'celebrate diversity and foster inclusivity'. The Indian Express. Retrieved on December 27, 2022 (https://indianexpress.com/article/cities/delhi/iit-d-to-set-up-office-to-celebrate-diversity-and-foster-inclusivity-7724084)
2. Gramsci introduced the concept of cultural hegemony in the Marxist framework. It refers to the dominance of a diverse society by the ruling class who manipulate the culture of that society—the beliefs and explanations, perceptions, values, and mores—so that the worldview of the ruling class becomes the accepted cultural norm. Thus, the socio-economic and political status quo are misrepresented as being natural, inevitable, and beneficial to all classes, rather than being contrived for the exclusive benefit to the ruling class.
3. Gramsci proposed a *strategic distinction* between two kinds of war. The war of position is an intellectual and cultural struggle to create a proletarian culture whose native value system counters the cultural hegemony of the bourgeoisie. Class distinctions are emphasized, changing the academic discourse and revolutionary organization. Then, in the war of manoeuver, popular and political support are mobilized for social revolution.
4. (Horkheimer, Critical Theory Selected Essays 1982, 244)
5. (Wilkerson 2020, 273)
6. (The New York Public Library 2020)
7. See: 'Isabel Wilkerson'. Isabel Wilkerson. Retrieved on February 15, 2022 (https://www.isabelwilkerson.com)
8. See: 'Caste and the Durban conference'. Ministry of External Affairs: Government of India. Retrieved on February 15, 2022 (https://www.mea.gov.in/articles-in-indian-media.htm?dtl/18479/Caste+and+the+Durban+conference)
9. (Wilkerson 2020, 176)
10. (Wilkerson 2020, 17)
11. (Wilkerson 2020, 24)
12. (Wilkerson 2020, 18)
13. (Wilkerson 2020, 19)
14. (Wilkerson 2020, 19)

15. (Wilkerson 2020, 26)
16. (Wilkerson 2020, 29)
17. (Wilkerson 2020, 25)
18. (Wilkerson 2020, 29)
19. (Wilkerson 2020, 74)
20. (Wilkerson 2020, 104)
21. (Wilkerson 2020, 268)
22. See: 'Africans in India: From Slaves to Generals and Rulers'. New York Public Library. Retrieved on February 15, 2022 (https://www.nypl.org/blog/2013/01/31/africans-india-slaves-generals-and-rulers). Also see: 'Indian Ocean and Middle Eastern Slave Trades'. Oxford Bibliographies. Retrieved on February 15, 2022 (https://www.oxfordbibliographies.com/view/document/obo-9780199846733/obo-9780199846733-0051.xml) and 'The story of East Africa's role in the transatlantic slave trade'. *The Conversation*. Retrieved on February 15, 2022 (https://theconversation.com/the-story-of-east-africas-role-in-the-transatlantic-slave-trade-43194)
23. (Levi 2002) When I first saw the PhD dissertation of Scott Levi being done at University of Wisconsin-Madison, I did not notice any mention about slavery in India before the Muslims. The dissertation was about slavery during Islam in India, and it was based on archives of that period available in the former USSR. But then a warning was issued by academic scholars that his work would play into the hands of 'Hindu activists' like me. The published version was adapted with a preamble saying that slavery pre-dates Islam in India because it is mentioned in the Vedic literature. However, that claim is incorrect because it is based on mistranslating the Vedic Sanskrit term 'dasu' as 'slave', which is an incorrect translation.
24. See: 'Caste Among Indian Muslims Is a Real Issue. So Why Deny Them Reservation?' *The Wire*. Retrieved on February 15, 2022 (https://thewire.in/caste/caste-among-indian-muslims-real-why-deny-reservation) and also 'Islam And Caste Inequality Among Indian Muslims'. Indian Dalit Muslims' Voice. Retrieved on February 15, 2022 (https://dalitmuslims.wordpress.com/2009/07/13/islam-and-caste-inequality-among-indian-muslims)
25. See: 'Debates on Muslim Caste in North India and Pakistan: from colonial ethnography to pasmanda mobilization'. *HAL Open Science*. Retrieved on February 15, 2022 (https://hal.archives-ouvertes.fr/hal-02697381) and also 'India's Muslim community under a churn: 85% backward Pasmandas up against 15% Ashrafs'. *The Print*. Retrieved on February 15, 2022 (https://theprint.in/opinion/indias-muslim-community-under-a-churn-85-backward-pasmandas-up-against-15-ashrafs/234599)
26. Spanish caste system: 'Spanish Caste System'. Nuestra Verdad Publicación. Retrieved on February 15, 2022 (https://www.nuestraverdad.com/post/

spanish-caste-system); Latin American caste system: 'Figure 1 - uploaded by Hector Y Adames'. ResearchGate. Retrieved on February 15, 2022 (https://www.researchgate.net/figure/Latin-American-Social-Caste-Pyramid-LASCP_fig1_262107699); Pakistan's caste system: (Barth 1956); China's urban caste system: (Tang and Yang 2008); Japan's caste system: "Japan's hidden caste of untouchables." *BBC* News. Retrieved on February 15, 2022 (https://www.bbc.com/news/world-asia-34615972).

27. (Wilkerson 2020, 76)
28. See, for example, Cox's 1948 book that caste is not race. 'Caste, Class, and Race'. Global Social Theory. Retrieved on February 15, 2022 (https://globalsocialtheory.org/concepts/caste-class-and-race)
29. (Wilkerson 2020, 106)
30. See: 'A social science centre engaged in major issues facing contemporary India and South Asia in an era of globalization'. Center de Sciences Humaines. Retrieved on December 27, 2022 (https://www.csh-delhi.com/about/institution)
31. See: 'Roland LARDINOIS'. Center de Sciences Humaines. Retrieved on December 27, 2022 (https://www.csh-delhi.com/team_member/roland-lardinois-2)
32. (OpenEdition 2011)
33. (OpenEdition 2011)
34. (Gill 2008)
35. (Gill 2008)
36. (S. Deshpande 2013)
37. (S. Deshpande 2013)
38. (S. Deshpande 2013)
39. (S. Deshpande 2013)
40. (S. Deshpande 2013)
41. (Subramanian 2015)
42. (Subramanian 2015)
43. (Subramanian 2015)
44. (Subramanian 2015)
45. (Subramanian 2015)
46. (Centre de Sciences Humaines 2019)
47. (Centre de Sciences Humaines 2019)
48. (Henry and Ferry 2017)
49. (University of Michigan Center for South Asian Studies 2016)
50. (Jordan B Peterson 2017)
51. See: 'Does biology explain why men outnumber women in tech?' The Conversation. Retrieved on December 27, 2022 (https://theconversation.com/does-biology-explain-why-men-outnumber-women-in-tech-82479)
52. (Henry and Ferry 2017)

53. (Henry and Ferry 2017)
54. (Henry and Ferry 2017)
55. See: 'South Asia Without Borders Seminar Series'. The Lakshmi Mittal and Family South Asia Institute at Harvard University. Retrieved on April 30, 2022 (https://mittalsouthasiainstitute.harvard.edu/event/south-asia-without-borders-seminar-series)
56. (Subramanian 2019, 23)
57. (Weber 1905)
58. See: 'Christianity's Meritocratic Dilemma: Reflections on Sandel's The Tyranny of Merit'. *Providence Magazine*. Retrieved on February 15, 2022 (https://providencemag.com/2021/11/christianitys-meritocratic-dilemma-reflections-michael-sandel-tyranny-of-merit/)
59. (Sandel 2020)
60. See: 'Michael Sandel: "The populist backlash has been a revolt against the tyranny of merit"'. *The Guardian*. Retrieved on February 15, 2022 (https://www.theguardian.com/books/2020/sep/06/michael-sandel-the-populist-backlash-has-been-a-revolt-against-the-tyranny-of-merit)
61. (Subramanian 2019, 27)
62. (Subramanian 2019, 28)
63. (Subramanian 2019, 31)
64. Unlike Britain, the mental and manual aspects of technical work are integrated in Germany, and students are expected to do intellectual, conceptual, abstract work along with physical tasks like carpentry and metal work. German engineering, in fact, prioritizes technique over theory. The engineer is first and foremost trained as a skilled technician.
65. (Subramanian 2019, 26)
66. (Malhotra 2022)
67. This is a slightly edited version from the article: (Malhotra 2022)
68. (Sambara 2021)
69. Larry Summers, president of Harvard, became controversial for saying that men and women had different kinds of aptitude. See: 'Why women are poor at science, by Harvard president'. *The Guardian*. Retrieved on February 15, 2022 (https://www.theguardian.com/science/2005/jan/18/educationsgendergap.genderissues)
70. (Sindwani 2020)
71. (Subramanian 2019, 260)
72. (Subramanian 2019, 268)
73. (Subramanian 2019, 293)
74. (Subramanian 2019, 299)
75. (Sambara 2021)
76. (Ambedkar King Study Circle USA 2020). Timestamps: 03:54 and 9:54.
77. (Sambara 2021)

78. (Subramanian 2019, 304)
79. (Subramanian 2019, 305)
80. (Kodaikanal International School 2021). Timestamp: 00:00:43-00:00:51.
81. (Subramanian 2019, 314)
82. (Subramanian 2019, 303)
83. Subramanian shows her true colors when she starts supporting the Kashmir separatists, Maqbool Bhatt and Afzal Guru, who were charged for the 2001 terrorist attack on the Indian Parliament. It is interesting that her criticism is echoed in the reports by the US Commission on International Religious Freedom labeling India as a Country of Concern because it allegedly suppresses religious freedom. Positioning herself with the USCIRF, she accuses Modi of violent attacks on Muslims and Dalits, the arrest of civil and human rights activists, and the killing of journalists. She does not believe that such things ever happened under previous governments. She also criticizes the Modi government for celebrating Sanskrit and establishing separate facilities for vegetarians and non-vegetarians, as though that is something contrary to lower caste interests.
84. (Subramanian 2019, 321)
85. (Sambara 2021)
86. (Sambara 2021)
87. (Higgins 2021)
88. (Equality Labs 2018a)
89. (North Star Fund 2017)
90. See: 'Dr. T.S.S. Rajan MD'. *U.S. News*. Retrieved on April 30, 2022 (https://health.usnews.com/doctors/tss-rajan-1225010)
91. See: 'Thenmozhi Soundararajan'. Virginia Tech. Retrieved on April 30, 2022 (https://ccc.ipg.vt.edu/Programs/forum/Thenmozhi.html)
92. (Equality Labs 2018a)
93. (Equality Labs 2018b). See p.39 of the Full Report.
94. (Badrinathan, et al. 2021)
95. (Badrinathan, et al. 2021)
96. (Pew Research Center 2021)
97. (Pew Research Center 2021)
98. (Metcalf and Rolfe 2010)
99. (Equality Labs 2018b)
100. See: 'A Historic Congressional Hearing on Caste in the US'. *The Wire*. Retrieved on February 15, 2022 (https://thewire.in/caste/a-historic-congressional-hearing-on-caste-in-the-us)
101. (R. Rao 2021)
102. See: 'Who We Invest In'. New Media Ventures. Retrieved on February 15, 2022 (https://www.newmediaventures.org/investments). See also: 'Equality Labs has 1 Investor, New Media Ventures'. *Crunchbase*. Retrieved

on February 15, 2022 (https://www.crunchbase.com/search/principal.investors/field/organizations/num_investors/equality-labs). And: https://mobile.twitter.com/by2kaafi/status/1247926029319987206. This tweet, which has been deleted, stated: 'New Media Ventures (NMV) is one Angel Investor in EqualityLabs. NMV has many investors of which one name is recognizable – Omidyar Network'.

103. (Equality Labs 2018b)
104. See: 'Thenmozhi Soundararajan'. Atlantic Fellows. Retrieved on April 30, 2022 (https://racialequity.atlanticfellows.org/fellow/thenmozhi-soundararajan); Also see: 'The Atlantic Institute'. *Rhodes Trust.* Retrieved on April 30, 2022 (https://www.rhodeshouse.ox.ac.uk/about/the-atlantic-institute)
105. See: 'Describing a system of oppression is not a slur'. *Scroll.in.* Retrieved on February 15, 2022 (https://scroll.in/article/902949/describing-a-system-of-oppression-is-not-a-slur-creator-of-smash-brahmanical-patriarchy-poster)
106. See: 'HAF Legal Team Writes to CDE to Investigate Assault Allegations'. HAF. Retrieved on February 15, 2022 (https://www.hinduamerican.org/press/haf-legal-team-writes-cde-investigate-assault-allegations)
107. See: 'Why We Must End Caste Oppression'. *Reappropriate.* Retrieved on February 15, 2022 (http://reappropriate.co/2018/05/why-we-must-end-caste-oppression/)
108. (Sudhakar, et al. 2022)
109. (Sudhakar, et al. 2022)
110. (Sudhakar, et al. 2022)
111. See: '2020.06.30 DFEH v. Cisco Systems, Et Al. Civil Complaint – FILED'. *Scribd.* Retrieved on February 15, 2022 (https://www.scribd.com/document/467774912/2020-06-30-DFEH-v-Cisco-Systems-Et-Al-Civil-Complaint-FILED)
112. (Rising Up With Sonali 2020). Timestamp: 8:01
113. (Rising Up With Sonali 2020). Timestamp: 9:05-9:41
114. See: 'Protecting Our People'. Cisco. Retrieved on February 15, 2022 (https://blogs.cisco.com/news/protecting-our-people). The case was dismissed in October 2020. But Cisco's defense included statements like the law doesn't say you can't discriminate based on caste!
115. (Mukherji 2021)
116. See: 'India's engineers have thrived in Silicon Valley. So has its caste system'. *The Washington Post.* Retrieved on February 15, 2022 (https://www.washingtonpost.com/technology/2020/10/27/indian-caste-bias-silicon-valley/)
117. BAPS stands for Bochasanwasi Akshar Purushottam Swaminarayan Sanstha.

118. See: 'Why Is Caste Inequality Still Legal in America?' *The New York Times*. Retrieved on February 15, 2022 (https://www.nytimes.com/2021/05/25/opinion/caste-discrimination-us-federal-protection.html)
119. See: 'American Colleges as beginning to recognize caste as a protected class'. *Quartz India*. Retrieved on February 15, 2022 (https://qz.com/india/2081765/us-universities-like-uc-davis-ban-indian-caste-system-on-campus/)
120. (Ambedkar King Study Circle USA 2020). Timestamp: 20:28.
121. (Ambedkar International Center (AIC) 2021)
122. (Ambedkar International Center (AIC) 2021)
123. (Ambedkar International Center (AIC) 2021)
124. (Sambara 2021)
125. See: 'Companies Have Promised $35 Billion Toward Racial Equity. Where Is the Money Going?' *The Wall Street Journal*. Retrieved on February 15, 2022 (https://www.wsj.com/articles/companies-have-promised-billions-toward-racial-equity-where-is-the-money-going-11608570864)
126. See: 'The Unfinished Business of Office Diversity Training'. *The Wall Street Journal*. Retrieved on February 15, 2022 (https://www.wsj.com/articles/the-unfinished-business-of-office-diversity-training-11608512401)
127. See: 'Diversity Has Become a Booming Business. So Where Are the Results?' *Time*. Retrieved on February 15, 2022 (https://time.com/5696943/diversity-business)
128. See: 'EEO Data Collections'. The U.S. Equal Employment Opportunity Commission. Retrieved on February 15, 2022 (https://www.eeoc.gov/employers/eeo-data-collections)
129. See: 'Statement on the Interpretation of Caste Within the Brandeis Nondiscrimination Policy'. Brandeis University. Retrieved on February 15, 2022 (https://www.brandeis.edu/human-resources/policies/discrimination/caste-statement.html)
130. See: 'UC Davis quietly added caste to its antidiscrimination policy. Will it cause others to do the same?' *San Francisco Chronicle*. Retrieved on February 15, 2022 (https://www.sfchronicle.com/california/article/UC-Davis-quietly-added-caste-to-its-16626845.php). Also see: 'California University Board unanimously votes to recognise protection from caste discrimination'. *The Hindu*. Retrieved on February 15, 2022 (https://www.thehindu.com/news/international/california-varsity-board-unanimously-votes-to-recognise-protection-from-caste-discrimination/article38328354.ece)
131. For Colby College, see: 'Maine's Colby College bans discrimination based on caste'. *AP*. Retrieved on February 15, 2022 (https://apnews.com/article/asia-education-discrimination-maine-south-asia-a4934667f35e70733e4986474a5021b0)

132. (Tejeda and Chahal 2021)
133. (Tejeda and Chahal 2021)
134. (Tejeda and Chahal 2021)
135. (Tejeda and Chahal 2021)
136. (Tejeda and Chahal 2021)
137. (R. Rao 2021)
138. (County of Santa Clara 2020)
139. (County of Santa Clara 2020)
140. See: 'Minutes'. County of Santa Clara Human Rights Commission. Retrieved on February 15, 2022 (http://sccgov.iqm2.com/Citizens/FileOpen.aspx?Type=12&ID=8723&Inline=True)
141. (Diya TV 2021). Timestamp: 05:28:20. The speaker identified herself as Nikhila Lakshmana.
142. (Ambedkar King Study Circle USA 2021)
143. See: 'Subject: Caste Based Discrimination in the United States'. County of Santa Clara. Retrieved on February 15, 2022 (http://sccgov.iqm2.com/Citizens/FileOpen.aspx?Type=4&ID=213125)
144. (Borgonjon 2017)
145. (Borgonjon 2017)
146. See: 'A Muslim student levelled false allegations against 3 professors at Dartmouth College in the USA just because they are Hindus: Details'. OpIndia. Retrieved on February 15, 2022 (https://www.opindia.com/2021/10/muslim-student-made-false-allegations-against-hindu-professors-in-usa)
147. (End Forced Arbitration 2022). Timestamp: 30:43-32:11.
148. (King 2018)
149. (Harvard University 2018)
150. (Yeung 2018)
151. (Varshney 2018)
152. (Varshney 2018)
153. (Varshney 2018)
154. (Varshney 2018)
155. (Varshney 2018)
156. (A. Deshpande 2018)
157. (A. Deshpande 2018)
158. (A. Deshpande 2018)
159. (A. Deshpande 2018)
160. (A. Deshpande 2018)
161. (A. Deshpande 2018)
162. (Harvard University 2018, 9). 'First is the role of technical education in caste formation. Rather than a space of universal knowledge where caste is no longer relevant, what we are seeing is the reconstitution of caste within and through the technical sciences. What this suggests is

that caste is both resilient within and foundational to the makeup of the most modern, apparently identity-free institutions. Second is how we understand the relationship between meritocracy and democracy. By bracketing out historically accumulated advantages and disadvantages, the notion of meritocracy, like that of a color-blind society, has come to service the reproduction of inequality. Of course, the ideal meaning of meritocracy as a system which corrects for historical privilege has not vanished. However, the divergence between its ideal meaning and its social life should call into question the easy assumption that meritocracy is indeed a leveller of opportunity'.

163. (The Lakshmi Mittal and Family South Asia Institute 2019); (Harvard University 2018, 15).
164. The complete video from which this has been derived is available at: (Infinity Foundation Official 2022)
165. See: 'American leadership in advancing the SDGs to achieve equity and sustainability'. Brookings. Retrieved on December 27, 2022 (https://www.brookings.edu/blog/up-front/2020/11/12/american-leadership-in-advancing-the-sdgs-to-achieve-equity-and-sustainability/
166. For instance, Carnegie Mellon University says that 'diversity, equity, and inclusion (DEI) are integral to CMU's Sustainability Initiative which builds on the UN's 17 Sustainable Development Goals (SDG), also known as Global Goals.' CMU's Professor Burcu Akinci said: 'We want to make [DEI] a part of their discipline—to make them much more aware and incorporate [DEI] into their thinking as they design, build, and manage teams in the future.' CMU has incorporated DEI practices into all levels from coursework to research to hiring. See: 'CEE DEI Committee Builds on SDG Goals'. Carnegie Mellon University. Retrieved on December 27, 2022 (https://www.cmu.edu/cee/news/news-archive/2021/02-2021-cee-dei-committee-builds-on-sdg-goals.html)
167. "Several different faculty members decried the jump in the number of administrators, telling Yale Daily News that academic bureaucracy expansion has been harmful to students and faculty and has also been unnecessarily burdensome and expensive." See: 'Yale Now Has More Administrators Than Undergrads Thanks To A Mammoth Bureaucracy'. The Federalist. Retrieved on December 27, 2022 (https://thefederalist.com/2021/11/11/yale-now-has-more-administrators-than-undergrads-thanks-to-a-mammoth-bureaucracy/)
168. See: 'Center for Sustainable Development and Global Competitiveness | About'. Stanford University. Retrieved on December 27, 2022 (https://sdgc.stanford.edu/about)
169. (UN DESA Sustainable Development 2022)
170. (Klima, Senra and De Backer 2021)
171. (Cottafava, et al. 2022)

172. (Klima, Senra and De Backer 2021)
173. See: 'The Role of the University in Environmental Sustainability'. Columbia Climate School. Retrieved on December 27, 2022 (https://news.climate.columbia.edu/2019/10/14/role-university-environmental-sustainability)
174. (Zizka, McGunagle and Clark 2021)
175. (Zizka, McGunagle and Clark 2021)
176. See: 'The World May Be Better Off Without ESG Investing'. Stanford Social Innovation Review. Retrieved on December 27, 2022 (https://ssir.org/articles/entry/the_world_may_be_better_off_without_esg_investing)
177. See: 'Academic Freedom Conference'. Stanford Graduate School of Business. Retrieved on December 27, 2022 (https://cli.stanford.edu/events/conference-symposium/academic-freedom-conference)
178. (Stanford Classical Liberalism Initiative 2022a)
179. (Stanford Classical Liberalism Initiative 2022b)
180. (Hoover Institution 2022)
181. (Stanford Classical Liberalism Initiative 2022c)
182. See: 'My latest editorial for @NatureHumanBehav on why ethics principles of benefit and harm should apply to all research about humans, not just primary research with human participants https://t.co/JP5Z1MKzi9'. Twitter. Retrieved on December 27, 2022 (https://twitter.com/KoustaStavroula/status/1562034181894455296)
183. (Stanford Classical Liberalism Initiative 2022c)
184. (Stanford Classical Liberalism Initiative 2022d)
185. (Stanford Classical Liberalism Initiative 2022d)
186. (The Wall Street Journal 2022)
187. (The Wall Street Journal 2022)
188. (Stanford Classical Liberalism Initiative 2022d)
189. See: 'Sustainable development becoming a higher education buzzword'. University World News. Retrieved on December 27, 2022 (https://www.universityworldnews.com/post.php?story=20120615171437704)
190. See: 'Higher Education Sustainability Initiative'. United Nations Department of Economic and Social Affairs (UNDESA). Retrieved on December 27, 2022 (https://sdgs.un.org/HESI)

Acknowledgments

We wish to thank several persons who have helped publish this volume and are facilitating the dissemination of its message widely. We are grateful to Ron Gupta, president, Pan-IIT, and Suresh Shenoy, past-president of Pan-IIT USA, for their support including strategic advice which we are pursuing as part of our ongoing work. Prakash Agrawal, Prakash Bhalerao, Vijay Bist, Arjun Bhagat and a few anonymous supporters in the Bay Area have pledged significant financial support for the foundation's various projects. Ravindra Shukla and Sarvajit Thakur have played important roles in helping us coordinate with important leaders to explain our mission and get broad support. Besides this recent help from the IIT community, we acknowledge Sashi Kejriwal's financial and other assistance over the past two decades.

Bibliography

Ambedkar International Center (AIC). 2021. *Cisco Caste Discrimination: AIC Press Release.* 2 March. Accessed February 15, 2022. https://ambedkarinternationalcenter.org/2021/03/cisco-caste-discrimination-aic-press-release/.

Ambedkar King Study Circle USA. 2020. *Practice of Caste in USA - HOW CASTE TRAVELS? by Dr.Ajantha Subramanian, Harvard University, USA.* 25 July. Accessed February 15, 2022. https://www.youtube.com/watch?v=gVweqgyGvKM.

—. 2021. *Santa Clara County HRC on Caste Discrimination.* 30 April. Accessed April 30, 2022. https://akscusa.org/santa-clara-county-hrc-on-caste-discrimination/.

Badrinathan, Sumitra, Devesh Kapur, Jonathan Kay, and Milan Vashnav. 2021. *Social Realities of Indian Americans: Results From the 2020 Indian American Attitudes Survey.* 9 June. Accessed 2022 15, February. https://carnegieendowment.org/2021/06/09/social-realities-of-indian-americans-results-from-2020-indian-american-attitudes-survey-pub-84667.

Barth, Fredrik. 1956. "Ecologic Relationships of Ethnic Groups in Swat, North Pakistan." *American Anthropologist* 58 (6): 1079-1089. https://www.jstor.org/stable/666295.

Borgonjon, David. 2017. *Artist Interview: Thenmozhi Soundararajan.* 20 April. Accessed February 15, 2022. https://www.eyebeam.org/five-questions-around-technology-and-stories-for-social-change/.

Centre de Sciences Humaines. 2019. *Odile HENRY.* 24 January. Accessed December 27, 2022. https://www.csh-delhi.com/team_member/odile-henry/.

Cottafava, Dario, Grazia Sveva Ascione, Laura Corazza, and Amandeep Dhir. 2022. "Sustainable development goals research in higher education institutions: An interdisciplinarity assessment through an entropy-based indicator." *Journal of Business Research* 151: 138-155. doi:https://doi.org/10.1016/j.jbusres.2022.06.050.

County of Santa Clara. 2020. *Receive report from Equity Labs relating to caste discrimination in Silicon Valley, and approve recommendations, if any.*

12 November. Accessed February 15, 2022. http://sccgov.iqm2.com/Citizens/Detail_LegiFile.aspx?ID=103782&highlightTerms=Caste.

Deshpande, Ashwini. 2018. "Meritocracy and Affirmative Action in India." *Harvard China Fund.* 8 May. Accessed May 15, 2022. https://hcf.fas.harvard.edu/wp-content/uploads/2018/05/Deshpande_Shanghai.pdf.

Deshpande, Satish. 2013. "Caste and Castelessness: Towards a Biography of the 'General Category'." *Economic and Political Weekly* 48 (15): 32-39. https://www.jstor.org/stable/23527121.

Diya TV. 2021. *EXCLUSIVE: Santa Clara County Human Rights Commission debates caste | Diya TV.* 30 April. https://www.youtube.com/watch?v=9b6KJptrArU.

End Forced Arbitration. 2022. *A Conversation on Caste Discrimination with Thenmozhi Soundararajan.* 19 April. Accessed April 30, 2022. https://www.youtube.com/watch?v=rXyzbWAuPWQ.

Equality Labs. 2018b. *Caste in the United States - Reviews.* Accessed April 30, 2022. https://www.equalitylabs.org/castesurvey/#reviews.

—. 2018a. *Mission.* Accessed February 15, 2022. https://www.equalitylabs.org/mission.

Gill, Rajesh. 2008. "Bourdieu in a Dual Context: India and France." *Sociological Bulletin* 57 (2): 288–95. http://www.jstor.org/stable/23620793.

Harvard University. 2018. "Abstracts for Feb Meritocracy Workshop." *Harvard University.* May. Accessed April 30, 2022. https://hcf.fas.harvard.edu/wp-content/uploads/2018/05/Abstracts-for-Feb-Meritocracy-Workshop.pdf.

Henry, Odile, and Mathieu Ferry. 2017. "When Cracking the JEE is not Enough, Processes of Elimination and Differentiation." *South Asia Multidiscipinary Academic Journal* 15. https://journals.openedition.org/samaj/4291.

Higgins, Michael. 2021. *Minority professor denied grants because he hires on merit: 'People are afraid to think'.* 24 November. Accessed February 15, 2022. https://nationalpost.com/news/canada/minority-professor-denied-grants-because-he-hires-on-merit-people-are-afraid-to-think.

Hoover Institution. 2022. *The BYO Show: China's Totalitarian Gridlock, a Woke "Mind Virus," and Futbal vs. Football.* 28 November. Accessed December 27, 2022. https://www.youtube.com/watch?v=BzuP3ZALE-c.

Horkheimer, Max. 1982. *Critical Theory Selected Essays.* New York: Continuum Publishing Corporation.

Infinity Foundation Official. 2022. *IIT Madras gives response to Harvard | Snakes in the Ganga.* 31 October. Accessed December 27, 2022. https://www.youtube.com/watch?v=Xbf-uEKrdMU.

Jordan B Peterson. 2017. *2017/08/08: James Damore and his Google Memo on Diversity (complete).* 9 August. Accessed December 27, 2022. https://www.youtube.com/watch?v=SEDuVF7kiPU.

King, Ruth. 2018. *Mindful of Race: Transforming Racism from the Inside Out.* Boulder, Colarado: Sounds True.

Klima, Noel, Juliana Martins Vasconcelos Senra, and Jasmine De Backer. 2021. *Higher Education Institutions (HEIs) and SDG 16: Inter- and transdisciplinary cooperation towards impact.* 25 December. Accessed December 27, 2022. https://f3magazine.unicri.it/?p=2312.

Kodaikanal International School. 2021. *Quad Talks I Politics of Meritocracy with Prof. Ajantha Subramanian '86.* 17 March. Accessed February 15, 2022. https://www.youtube.com/watch?v=xNDM6aYx7uM.

Levi, Scott C. 2002. "Hindus beyond the Hindu Kush: Indians in the Central Asian slave trade." *Journal of the Royal Asiatic Society* 12 (3): 277-288.

Malhotra, Rajiv. 2022. *The Peer-Review Cartel.* 3 February. Accessed April 30, 2022. https://www.outlookindia.com/website/story/the-peer-review-cartel/222822.

Metcalf, Hilary, and Heather Rolfe. 2010. "Caste discrimination and harassment in Great Britain." *National Institute of Economic and Social Research.* December. https://www.niesr.ac.uk/wp-content/uploads/2021/10/caste-discrimination.pdf.

Mukherji, Anahita. 2021. *California's Legal Ground in Battling Caste Discrimination Takes Centre Stage in Historic Cisco Case.* 10 March. Accessed February 15, 2022. https://thewire.in/caste/cisco-case-caste-discrimination-silicon-valley-ambedkar-organisations.

North Star Fund. 2017. *North Star Fund Rapid Response Grants 2016-17.* 8 November. Accessed February 15, 2022. https://northstarfund.org/2017/11/north-star-fund-rapid-response-grants-2016-17/.

OpenEdition. 2011. *The Making of Indian Engineers: From the Colonial Period through the Present.* 24 October. Accessed December 27, 2022. https://www.openedition.org/9583?lang=en.

Pew Research Center. 2021. *4. Attitudes about caste.* 29 June. Accessed December 27, 2022. https://www.pewresearch.org/religion/2021/06/29/attitudes-about-caste/.

Rao, Raj. 2021. *Exclusive: Santa Clara County Human Rights Commission to hold hearing on caste.* 29 April. Accessed February 15, 2022. https://diyatvusa.com/2021/04/29/exclusive-santa-clara-county-human-rights-commission-to-hold-hearing-on-caste/.

Rising Up With Sonali. 2020. *How India's Caste Discrimination Made it to the USA.* 21 July. Accessed February 15, 2022. https://vimeo.com/440440045.

Sambara, Sraavya. 2021. *Caste and Colonialism Beyond the Subcontinent: An Interview with Ajantha Subramanian.* 1 September. Accessed

February 15, 2022. https://harvardpolitics.com/caste-and-colonialism-beyond-the-subcontinent-an-interview-with-ajantha-subramanian/.

Sandel, Michael J. 2020. *The Tyranny of Merit: What's Become of the Common Good?* Farrar, Straus and Giroux.

Sindwani, Prerna. 2020. *India tops the world in producing female graduates in STEM but ranks 19th in employing them.* 28 February. Accessed April 30, 2022. https://www.businessinsider.in/careers/news/india-tops-the-world-in-producing-female-graduates-in-stem-but-ranks-19th-in-employing-them/articleshow/74117413.cms.

Stanford Classical Liberalism Initiative. 2022d. *Academic Freedom in STEM with Jerry Coyne, Luana Maroja, Anna Krylov, Mimi St Johns.* 19 November. Accessed December 27, 2022. https://www.youtube.com/watch?v=5t_OGufHgOA.

—. 2022c. *Is Woke Science the Only Science Allowed in Academia.* 22 December. Accessed December 27, 2022. https://www.youtube.com/watch?v=SEHqk5CoUX0.

—. 2022a. *Opening Remarks by John H. Cochrane.* 19 November. Accessed December 27, 2022. https://www.youtube.com/watch?v=Tiao3M1-3k8.

—. 2022b. *Why It Has Gotten Harder to Find the Truth with Jonathan Haidt.* 19 November. Accessed December 27, 2022. https://www.youtube.com/watch?v=KIsN71aTICA.

Subramanian, Ajantha. 2015. "Making Merit: The Indian Institutes of Technology and the Social Life of Caste." *Comparative Studies in Society and History* 57 (2). https://www.cambridge.org/core/journals/comparative-studies-in-society-and-history/article/abs/making-merit-the-indian-institutes-of-technology-and-the-social-life-of-caste/C776AC2172B4FF45F87C130C45FA1C1A.

—. 2019. *The Caste of Merit.* Cambridge, MA: Harvard University Press.

Sudhakar, Prasiddha, John Farmer, Joel Finkelstein, Parth Parihar, Lee Jussim, and Denver Riggleman. 2022. *Anti-Hindu Disinformation: A Case Study of Hinduphobia on Social Media.* Miller Center for Policing Excellence and Community Resilience, Rutgers University, New Brunswick: July. Accessed December 27, 2022. https://millercenter.rutgers.edu/wp-content/uploads/2022/07/Hinduphobia-NC-Labs_6.22.22.pdf.

Tang, Wenfang, and Qing Yang. 2008. "The Chinese Urban Caste System in Transition." *The China Quarterly* (Cambridge University Press) (196): 759-779. http://www.jstor.org/stable/20192266.

Tejeda, Amanda, and Manmit Singh Chahal. 2021. "Resolution #21-01: RESOLUTION CALLING FOR CAL POLY AND THE CALIFORNIA STATE UNIVERSITY (CSU) TO INCLUDE

CASTE IN ANTI-DISCRIMINATORY POLICY." *CalPoly.* 4 March. Accessed February 15, 2022. https://www.asi.calpoly.edu/wp-content/uploads/2021/03/21-01-Resolution-Call-for-CP-and-CSU-to-Include-Caste-in-the-Anti-Discriminatory-Policy_BODappr.pdf.

The Lakshmi Mittal and Family South Asia Institute. 2019. *Talent and Meritocracy in China and India.* 16 April. Accessed May 15, 2022. https://mittalsouthasiainstitute.harvard.edu/talent-and-meritocracy-in-india-and-china-february-2018-workshop/.

The New York Public Library. 2020. *Caste in America: Isabel Wilkerson with John Dickerson | LIVE from NYPL.* 6 August. Accessed February 15, 2022. https://www.youtube.com/watch?v=FxpouTYfJKY.

The Wall Street Journal. 2022. *The Stanford Guide to Acceptable Words.* 19 December. Accessed December 27, 2022. https://www.wsj.com/articles/the-stanford-guide-to-acceptable-words-elimination-of-harmful-language-initiative-11671489552.

UN DESA Sustainable Development. 2022. *HESI+10 Global Forum.* 2022 July. Accessed December 27, 2022. https://www.youtube.com/watch?v=yLffPtpFMmU.

Varshney, Ashutosh. 2018. "Democracy and Meritocracy." *Harvard China Fund.* 8 May. Accessed May 15, 2022. https://hcf.fas.harvard.edu/wp-content/uploads/2018/05/Varshney-Abstract-Shanghai.pdf.

Weber, Max. 1905. *The Protestant Ethic and the Spirit of Capitalism.* Pantianos Classics.

Wilkerson, Isabel. 2020. *Caste: The Origins of Our Discontent.* New York: Random House.

Yeung, Bernard. 2018. "Notes on Meritocracy: Insights from Tang's Civil Servant Exam and Poetry." *Harvard China Fund.* 1 May. Accessed May 15, 2022. https://hcf.fas.harvard.edu/wp-content/uploads/2018/05/Yeung-Bernie-For-May-2018-b.pdf.

Zizka, Laura, Doreen M. McGunagle, and Patti J. Clark. 2021. "Sustainability in science, technology, engineering and mathematics (STEM) programs: Authentic engagement through a community-based approach." *Journal of Cleaner Production* 279. doi:https://doi.org/10.1016/j.jclepro.2020.123715.

INDEX

C

D

Y

Z

Books by BluOne Ink

Kali Imprint

Sri Aurobindo & the Literary Renaissance of India | Pariksith Singh
ISBN: 9788194954781 | ₹995

Sri Aurobindo and Philosophy | Pariksith Singh
ISBN: 9789392209017 | ₹995

Somewhere Among the Stars | Adi Varuni
ISBN: 9789392209215 | ₹395

The Eternal Feminine | Dr Alok Pandey
ISBN: 9788194954774 | ₹699

Integral Education | Partho
ISBN: 9788194954705 | ₹499

Hindutva: Origin, Evolution and Future | Aravindan Neelakandan
ISBN: 978-93-92209-06-2 | ₹995

BluPrint Imprint

Identity's Last Secret | Makarand R. Paranjape
ISBN: 9788194954798 | ₹1495

Swayam Se Parichay (in Hindi) | Pariksith Singh
ISBN: 9789392209185 | ₹195

Chhutti Ke Din (bilingual in Hindi and Rajasthani) | Pariksith Singh
ISBN: 9789392209024 | ₹699

Anjali Geetan Ri (in Rajasthani) | Ikraam Rajasthani
ISBN: 9789392209277 | ₹250

Jana Awjanar Majhe (in Bengali) | Bimal Chakravartty
ISBN: 9789392209277 | ₹250

The Eternal Gene and Other Tales of Malaise | Ankush Sam Thorpe
ISBN: 978-93-92209-14-7 | ₹495

All Stray Dogs Go to Heaven | Krishna Candeth
ISBN: 978-93-92209-08-6 | ₹695

Occam Imprint

Confidence Cures | Lt Gen. S. B. Sehajpal and Mrs Kiran Sehajpal
ISBN: 9789392209260 | ₹495

War Despatches 1971 | Brigadier B. S. Mehta
ISBN: 9789392209123 | ₹899

March to Justice | Navdeep Singh and Frank Rosenblatt
ISBN: 9788194954712 | ₹995

The Fighting Fourth | Brigadier Jasbir Singh, SM,
ISBN: 9788194954750 | ₹699

Once Upon a Time in RIMC | Brigadier Jasbir Singh, SM
ISBN: 9788194954729 | ₹250

Design: A Business Case | Brigitte Borja de Mozota and Steinar Valade-Amland
ISBN: 9788194954743 | ₹795

MRA Made Simple: Seriously? | Pariksith Singh, MD and Lynda Dilts-Benson
ISBN: 9781954261006 | $29.99

Compliance Made Simple: Seriously? | Pariksith Singh, MD and Lynda Dilts-Benson
ISBN: 9781954261013 | $55.99

Snakes in the Ganga: Breaking India 2.0 | Rajiv Malhotra and Vijaya Viswanathan
ISBN: 978-93-92209-09-3 | ₹895

Life of an Industani: Six Degrees of Separation | Shiv Kunal Verma

ISBN: 978-93-92209-15-4 | ₹995

Grit to Glory | Brig. B.S. Mehta

ISBN: 978-93-92209-29-1 | ₹895

Forthcoming Titles by BluOne Ink

Seeing with Hands | Jinan K. B.

ISBN: 978-93-92209-00-0

Of Newtons and Apples | Dr Abhishek Kumar

ISBN: 978-93-92209-24-6

The Power of Future Machines | Rajiv Malhotra, T. N. Sudarshan and Manogna Sastry (Eds)

ISBN: 978-93-92209-33-8

The Quest | Aparajita Barai

ISBN: 978-93-92209-23-9